TEMPE, DU STADT MEINER TRÄUME

TEMPE, DU STADT MEINER TRÄUME

STUDIES IN PSYCHOGEOGRAPHY

Occasional Papers no. 1

GREGORY STEPHENSON

Ober-Limbo Verlag

Grateful acknowledgement is made to Brent Blazek & Drew S. Swenhaugen, editors of *The Maple/Ash Review* in which *"From the Burning"* and *"Unreal City: The Ravaging of Tempe"* first appeared.

Published by Ober-Limbo Verlag
Heidelberg, Germany

ISBN 978-87-971569-1-9

Cover design & layout by Birgit Stephenson

"Tempe where Jove
griev'd that day"

John Keats
"On a Dream"

CONTENTS

DREAM DATA

DREAM DIARIES BEGUN IN ODENSE, DENMARK ON 19 APRIL 1974

7 Aug 74: From 1218 S. Farmer Avenue no. 3 north to 10th Street. Turn east on 10th, cross Mill Avenue to Tempe Center. Return to S. Farmer Ave. with mighty strides then soar above trees and rooftops.

15 Sep 74: The year is 1935. I stand gazing at the r.r. tracks at 6th Street & S. Farmer Ave. Apply for & get job at Hayden Flour Mill. Travel south on Mill Ave. to Hayden Library on ASU campus. Then, to green wooden cabins of 1920s autocourt (formerly Holford's Cabins) at 2nd Street & Ash Avenue.

17 Sep 75: Return to Tempe & rent 1218 S. Farmer Avenue, no. 3.

7 Apr 76: On the ASU campus, I attend an eloquent speech delivered by Henry Miller.

30 Jan 77: Walking south on S. Maple Avenue between 10th and 13th Streets, delighting to be there. Pass waterfall, cross river, arrive at 1214 S. Farmer Avenue. I feel drawn to Tempe as if by a magnetic current.

7 Feb 77: I ride north in a deuce-and-a-half (two and a half ton truck) along S. Farmer Avenue to 10th Street where we turn right (east) and proceed to Mill Avenue.

8 Feb 77: Walk south on Ash Avenue south of 10th Street, admiring the houses. I am very happy to be here. I resolve to become mayor of Tempe.

12 Feb 77: Smoking reefer inside an apartment at 1218 S. Farmer Avenue.

27 Feb 77: Tempe Butte. ASU campus.

26 Mar 77: I teach a class in the Language & Literature building at ASU.

11 Apr 77: ASU. A large auditorium.

10 May 77: From the south side of Tempe Butte, I look down on the ASU campus. I sigh with gladness and satisfaction to be there.

21 Aug 77: Corridors of the Language & Literature building on the ASU campus.

27 Aug 77: On the south bank of the dry Salt River, near the base of the Mill Avenue Bridge.

16 Oct 77: Exultant to be living in a cabin at the old autocourt at 2nd Street and Ash Avenue.

25 Nov 77: Feeling exalted to be in Tempe, but saddened to see that some of the old territorial buildings along Mill Avenue have been demolished. Relieved to see that the Casa Loma and the Hut are still standing. And the Salt River is running!

15 Feb 78: Industrial Park Avenue. Even in these, bland, banal surroundings I find it very agreeable to be in Tempe.

24 Feb 78: Walking south on west side of Mill Avenue between 9th and 10th Streets. I remark to my companion how very much I like Tempe & how glad I am to be there. This is my place, I say, my real home. We stop for an ice-cream at the Dairy Queen on 10th and Mill Avenue.

17 Apr 78: I stroll the streets of Tempe, sighing with longing to live in one of the houses there. At last, I find a bungalow just north of the Dairy Queen at 10th Street and Mill Avenue.

14 May 78: In west Phoenix, trying to find a way to get to Tempe. I tell a companion how intensely I am attracted to Tempe.

15 May 78: Riding south across the Mill Avenue Bridge & onto Mill Avenue. I enter Tempe in a state of excitement and exaltation. I intend to apply for a job at the Hayden Flour Mill.

21 May 78: Across Mill Avenue from the Dairy Queen at 10th & Mill, I call the attention of my companions to the appealing view to the west along 10th Street.

26 Jul 78: On Wilson Street between 12th and 13th Streets, I point out attractive houses to my companions.

30 Jul 78: Attend a backyard party at a house on the south side 13th Street, just west of Wilson Street.

16 Dec 78: Standing on the west side of Mill Avenue at 10th Street, looking west. I sigh in my soul with happiness at being here. I walk 10th to S. Farmer Avenue, then back to the Dairy Queen where I buy a double ice cream cone.

28 Jan 79: I am pleased & relieved to see that the old territorial buildings along Mill Avenue have not been razed.

6 Feb 79: ASU campus, Cady Mall. Sitting in sunlight on a stone planter.

21 Mar 79: Moving back into an apartment at 1214 or 1218 S. Farmer Avenue. A freight train moans and rumbles along the r.r. tracks just to the east of Farmer. I am so moved to hear it that I can't speak. Later, I rhapsodize about the quaint beauty of the old houses on Farmer.

23 May 79: Packing, leaving our apartment on S. Farmer Avenue. Driving north along Farmer, already determined to return to Tempe. Turn right (east) on University Drive, then left (north) on Mill Avenue.

4 Aug 79: Riding a bus southward along Mill Avenue, past 10th Street where I grieve to see an old house being demolished. Descend from bus & stand gazing with deep joy & excitement at the houses.

18 Aug 79: I am enraged to see that along 13th Street between Ash Avenue & Roosevelt Street, many houses have been razed. Yet, for me enough of mystery and attraction still remains.

30 Aug 79: In the distance, I can see Tempe. With a shout of joy, I set off running toward it.

18 Sep 79: We move into an apartment on S. Farmer Avenue. It is wonderful to have returned.

26 Sep 79: Walking along the east side of Mill Avenue, cross at 10th Street & walk west on 10th, stepping across the r.r. tracks. I am deeply pleased to be there.

24 Nov 79: Descend from bus onto sidewalk of East 5th Street. I'm glad to be there.

6 Dec 79: Apartments at S. Farmer Avenue. Excited to be there.

8 Dec 79: I stand at 10th Street & S. Farmer Avenue, feeling a thrill of excitement.

27 Dec 79: Seeking an apartment at 1214 S. Farmer Avenue.

24 Jan 80: I stroll the cement sidewalk of Tempe Center, happy & marvelling at the shops. Then, drive past Tempe Beach Park & the Hayden Flour Mill for a beer at The Hut.

9 Mar 80: I view houses on east side of S. Farmer Avenue just north of 13th Street. I am swept with magnetic attraction.

18 Mar 80: On foot, somewhere distant from Tempe, trying to get there.

DEPART DENMARK 31 MARCH 1980. RESIDE IN TEMPE JUNE 1980 TO AUGUST 1981.

29 Dec 80: I heap invective on the Tempe City Council for their callous destruction of the old territorial buildings & entire neighborhoods of charming houses. Vandals!

22 Jan 80: I soar above 10th Street, turn left (south) on S. Farmer Avenue, then right (west) on 13th Street.

18 Mar 81: I discover an old & unknown area of the ASU campus. With joy, I fly back to our apartment at 124 E. Sixth Street.

9 Apr 81: Allen Ginsberg reads his poems on the ASU campus.

1 Sep 81: We have returned again to Tempe & live happily in a house on the s.w. corner of 9th Street & Ash Avenue. (Dreamed on the night before our departure to Denmark.)

RETURN TO DENMARK 3 SEPTEMBER 1981.

6 Oct 81: Tempe Center. I extol to my companion all the many good things to be found in Tempe.

16 Dec 81: Walking east on the north side of 6th Street between Mill Avenue & S. Forest Avenue. I must find work so that I can remain in Tempe.

4 Feb 82: I walk along north side of 13th Street toward S. Farmer Avenue, admiring the houses, tingling with excitement & a sense of the mystery of Tempe.

16 May 82: A beer at the Bandersnatch at 125 E. 5th Street.

20 May 82: On the second floor of a building adjacent to Changing Hands Bookstore at 414 S. Mill Avenue, I find still hanging on the wall an abandoned calendar from 1923 turned to the month of February.

2 Jul 82: From 13th Street, turn left (north) on S. Farmer Avenue. Appalled to see that 1950s subdivision houses on both sides of the street are being razed. Multi-storied apartment complexes are to be built on the properties.

14 Nov 82: Roaming 2nd and 3rd Streets on the west side of Mill Avenue. Admiring the old houses & ranting to a companion against the relentless engulfment of old Tempe by blandness & banality.

7 Dec 82: The Desert Flower Café on 5th Street, explaining to owners why I had to leave Tempe & how intensely I long to return.

1 Jan 83: I have returned to live in an apartment at 1214 S. Farmer Avenue. Speaking to the landlord, I praise the marvellous prospect before our eyes: the distant mountains, the handsome, quirky old houses. Ride in automobile to 2nd Street, west of Mill Avenue, admiring en route the old buildings, the houses & full grown trees.

13 Jan 83: Returned to Tempe. Attentive appreciation of the ASU campus.

25 Jan 83: I try to persuade landlord to allow me to rent apartment at 1214 or 1218 S. Farmer Avenue. By way of argument, I tell him of my many night dreams of Tempe.

28 Jan 83: Standing at the bus station on East 5th Street, I am filled with sorrow at having to leave Tempe. I walk onto Mill Avenue, taking a last, sad, lingering look at the town, the buildings, the mill, the bridge.

28 Feb 83: I study the earth of a vacant lot south of & near the base of Tempe Butte.

4 May 83: Riding to Tempe to hear a poetry reading.

1 Jun 83: Driving toward Tempe.

6 Nov 83: The Valley Art Theatre is being demolished to be replaced by a new commercial building. At the far end of the ruins only the screen remains. I rail & lament.

22 Nov 83: Riding in a car, approaching Tempe. Choking with emotion, I recount to companions my deep, intense attraction to Tempe.

10 Dec 83: I enter the Hayden Library on the ASU campus & admire the familiar interior. After exchanging pleasantries with a friendly librarian, I exit & stand gazing with profound pleasure & satisfaction at the features of the city around me. I sense the mystery of old Tempe & feel tingling within me a current of excitement.

9 Jul 84: Standing on east side of Mill Avenue at 5th Street, I expound at length to companions about the history of the old buildings of the downtown.

9 Dec 84: I return to Tempe & view the apartments at 1214 & 1218 S. Farmer Avenue. I note with pleasure that all remains intact. The wonderful old Judd House at 1208 S. Farmer Avenue still stands. This is the locus of my soul & my heart.

24 Dec 84: I am pleased to find employment at a small factory on the east side of Mill Avenue at 2nd Street.

11 Jan 85: I ride a bus southward across Tempe Bridge & into the downtown. I am euphoric, ecstatic. I descend from the bus onto a sidewalk on the west side of Mill Avenue at 4th Street.

16 Jan 85: Riding a bus westward on 13th Street, west of Mill Avenue. I point out to companions certain interesting houses & tell them that

there will be many more such to see when we turn right (north) onto S. Farmer Avenue.

5 Feb 85: I'm looking for an apartment to rent, roaming the quarter on the east side of Mill Avenue at 3rd Street. There are a number of individual & imaginative small wooden houses there. I feel a physical thrill of excitement.

16 Feb 85: Walking S. Farmer Avenue near 13th Street. I exult to be there. I remark to my companion how wonderful it is & now that I have returned, I must never again leave.

7 Apr 85: Ah, sitting in the dark in the Valley Art Theatre!

26 Apr 85: Standing before the magazine rack at Low Cost grocery store (formerly El Rancho) at Tempe Center, I am very pleased to see again magazines such as *The Atlantic, Harper's* and *Esquire.*

29 Apr 85: Riding a bus eastward on 10th Street, east of Mill Avenue. My goal is the ASU campus.

8 Jun 85: I walk past the large, handsome house on the n.w. corner of Ash Avenue & 10th Street. Then, I rush to 1214 S. Farmer Avenue where I have learned that there is an apartment for rent.

9 Jun 85: Friends pick us up in their car. They will drive us to Tempe.

31 Jul 85: Standing on the north side of 13th Street, near Wilson, gazing with pleasure upon the charming houses. I tell my companion that I've never wished to live anywhere else than in Tempe, yet I succeeded in doing so only for such a brief time.

17 Sep 85: Walking north on the east side of Maple Avenue between 10th Street & University Drive, noting with approval the irregular

configurations of houses, the slightly unkempt, bohemian ambiance of the neighborhood.

10 Oct 85: In the student bookstore located in the Memorial Union Building, I encounter & speak to Professor Nicholas Salerno, who remembers me.

24 Oct 85: Walking in the alley that runs from north to south just east of Maple Avenue between University Dr. & 9th Street, behind "the hovel" at 821 and a half S. Maple in which we once lived.

13 Dec 85: Sitting on a bench on Cady Mall, ASU campus. Then sitting in the Valley Art Theatre.

6 Jan 86: Walking west on the north side of 10th Street in the direction of S. Farmer Avenue where we have rented an apartment. I rejoice to be in Tempe again & regard with close attention & keen appreciation the houses I pass.

23 Feb 86: I stand on the west side of Mill Avenue at 10th Street (north side of the street.) I find all that I behold so charming & so appealing. I can see all the way down 10th Street to S. Farmer Avenue.

5 Apr 86: Walking the neighborhood south of Apache Boulevard between College Avenue & McAllister Avenue. I feel excitement & interest. Even a vacant lot delights me with its charm.

2 Jul 86: Entering the Valley Art Theatre, I pause to look north along Mill Avenue. I sigh to see that so few original, authentic buildings yet remain (so many having been razed & replaced.)

26 Jul 86: I have returned to live in Tempe & am walking along the west side of Mill Avenue just north of 10th Street. I pass the Dairy Queen on my left & later Pete's Fish & Chips. And then, ah, dear old Rundle's!

22 Sep 86: Walking north in the alley that runs between 13th Street & 12th Street & between S. Farmer Avenue & Wilson Street. Beguiled, I extol to a companion the individual character of the houses & long leafy backyards that we see about us.

25 Oct 86: I arrive in Tempe at dusk & walk north along Mill Avenue, crossing from the east to the west side of the street, planning to drop in Changing Hands Bookstore. But overcome with joy at having returned to Tempe, I fall to the sidewalk, sobbing & weeping.

13 Dec 86: I am walking on the west side of Mill Avenue, approaching 13th Street. I admire the houses & rejoice to be there.

1 Jan 87: I am in the Language & Literature building on the ASU campus, looking for Professor Salerno's office. I have just returned to Tempe & want to inquire about a teaching job.

7 Jan 87: Hoping to move back into an apartment at 1214 or 1218 S. Farmer Avenue for a monthly rental fee of 150 dollars.

8 Feb 87: In quiet joy, I sit watching a film in the Valley Art Theatre.

14 Mar 87: Just returned to Tempe & moved into apartment at 1214 S. Farmer Avenue. I walk the grounds & admire the Judd house at 1208 S. Farmer Ave.

6 Apr 87: I have rented an apartment on the west side of Mill Avenue between 10th & 13th Streets. I am well pleased. I walk the nearby streets, feeling their mystery.

27 Apr 87: Walking the grounds of the apartments at 1214 & 1218 S. Farmer Avenue & in the stony alley that runs from 13th to 12th Street & between S. Farmer Avenue & Wilson Street.

10 May 87: Walking east on University Drive across the street from the student dormitories.

21 Sep 87: The earth of Tempe: I bend down to inspect it closely, savoring the sight of the soil & pebbles. I feel the enchantment, the attraction of the very ground here.

22 Oct 87: Returned to Tempe & looking for a place to live. Driven north along S. Farmer Avenue to University Drive, then a right turn (east) followed by another right turn (south) onto Ash Avenue thence to 10th Street & right again on S. Farmer Avenue. I am elated to view the houses on either side of the street. My voice breaking with emotion, I tell my companion that my dearest wish is to live here in this area to which I am so profoundly & ardently attached.

12 Nov 87: Standing on the sidewalk in front of the apartments at 1214 & 1218 S. Farmer Avenue. I study carefully the walls & windows of the houses facing the street, behind which I can see certain of the apartments in the rear. I sob & say aloud: "Oh, I wish I lived here!"

30 Nov 87: No vacancies are to be found among the apartments at 1214 & 1218 S. Farmer Avenue. I will search for a rental to the north along S. Farmer Avenue.

16 Feb 88: Rent an apartment at 1214 S. Farmer Avenue.

16 Mar 88: Sitting in a restaurant in Tempe sensing the mystery of the city all around me, feeling within me that familiar tingle of excitement.

19 Mar 88: Walking a street in Tempe, I turn my attention to the distant mountains. They are intensely colored, vibrant as if with an inner life or energy.

24 Mar 88: S. Roosevelt Street & Broadway Road. Walk north to 13th Street, then onto S. Farmer Avenue. How appealing, how attractive the houses are! I am sighing & sobbing with longing to be here, to live here.

5 May 88: I am walking east on the north side of 13th Avenue between Ash Avenue & Maple Avenue. I turn right (south) on Mill Avenue & discover a very agreeable & mysterious quarter of the city that I have never before visited, with handsome old houses & large redbrick factory buildings dating from the 1920s.

22 June 88: Walking south on S. Farmer Avenue just s. of University Drive. I gaze enraptured at the houses & babble enthusiastically of them to my companions. I am struck with wonder to see it all. "This is the only place I would ever wish to live," I remark.

1 Jul 88: At ASU, I am trying to find Professor Salerno in hopes of getting a teaching job.

11 Jul 88: I'm standing near the fountain on Orange Mall on the ASU campus. I have to attend an appointment with the Career Services office. I study details of the fountain & am suddenly overcome with emotion to be there.

29 Jul 88: We stand on the site of the apartments at 1214 & 1218 S. Farmer Avenue. The buildings have all been demolished, only vague traces of where the buildings once stood can be seen in the dirt.

17 Oct 88: The Language & Literature building on the ASU campus. I'm working as a part-time instructor with the English Department at ASU, hoping to establish myself as a person of substance in the eyes of my colleagues.

28 Oct 88: Cross Tempe Bridge onto Mill Avenue. I mourn to see that many of the old territorial buildings have been demolished. Yet still,

standing on the sidewalk on Mill Avenue, I feel that strange, familiar physical & psychic excitement, that gravitational attraction to Tempe.

7 Nov 88: Walking westward on 10th Street west of Mill Avenue. To a companion, I expatiate at length & with much enthusiasm about the houses we see, directing attention to particular architectural details.

5 Dec 88: Riding west in a car on 10th Street west of Mill Avenue, passing Maple & Ash, heading for S. Farmer Avenue. I praise the houses we are seeing for their individual character. I sigh with the desire to be here & remain here.

30 Jan 89: The Language and Literature building on the ASU campus. I'm inquiring there for a job.

31 Jan 89: We have rented our former apartment (no. 3) at 1218 S. Farmer Avenue. I open the door, enter the bare apartment. I'm deeply moved to have returned to this space, this place. I savor the sense of continuity with the past, together with the sense of a new beginning.

13 Feb 89: Riding a bus southward along Mill Avenue, past University Drive, past 10th Street. I look wistfully out the window, then sob with yearning to return, to be there.

29 Mar 89: We find a rental apartment in that quarter south of E. Apache Boulevard, to the south of the ASU campus.

31 May 89: I'm taking a class at ASU & looking for an apartment. On Wilson Avenue just north of 13th Street I come upon a small house for rent. This is a perfect place, just what we have always wanted.

4 Jul 89: I rush along E. Apache Boulevard, en route to an appointment for a job interview.

28 Jul 89: Sitting in a café on the west side of Mill Avenue near 4th Street. I am depressed to see how few of the original, authentic old buildings yet remain on Mill Avenue. Then, to Tempe Center.

15 Nov 89: I receive a book of photographs of Tempe, causing me to feel sharp nostalgia & sorrow. I long to return there.

22 Nov 89: Walking north at dusk on the east side of Mill Avenue, at 7th Street. My companion & I take pleasure in the beauty of palm trees & the view we have of distant mountains.

24 Nov 89: Browsing in Changing Hands Bookstore at 414 Mill Avenue.

27 Nov 89: Drinking beer in hallowed Parry's Bar at 412 Mill Avenue. Then walk the dry sandy bed of the Salt River.

15 Dec 89: I walk north on S. Farmer Avenue from just north of Broadway Road. As I reach 13th Street, I feel exhilaration & joyous anticipation. I will soon be approaching the enchanted zone at 1214 & 1218 S. Farmer Avenue.

16 Jan 90: Walking among the streets & alleys in the quarter of the city north of University Drive, east of Mill Avenue & west of College Avenue: Myrtle Avenue, Forest Avenue, 7th Street, 6th Street. I feel keen excitement to see the houses & apartments there but am overcome with sorrow & frustration knowing I can't live there because I have no job, no money & my education & experience possess so little commercial value.

24 Jan 90: Wandering streets of the Maple/Ash district, admiring & coveting the houses there. I remark that if I were wealthy I would unhesitatingly buy one of the houses there. Later, at Ash Avenue & 10th Street, a gathering of nearly 20 people protesting proposed demolition of houses in this area by the Tempe City Council. A dreadful, depressing possibility. I inquire of a man whether he knows of an apartment for rent in this neighborhood.

31 Jan 90: Seeking to rent an apartment at 1214 or 1218 S. Farmer Avenue. Our former apartment at 1218 no. 3 is for rent, but I haven't got a job yet. We must wait. We meet two friendly young tenants of the apartments & are invited for dinner. I offer to walk to the 7-11 store on Ash Street near University to buy a few quarts of beer. That will be a most pleasant walk for me. I will see again the WPA sidewalks of dear memory.

27 Feb 90: I take a taxi into Tempe, ask driver to let me off at 10th Street & Ash Avenue. I have come to Tempe to look for a job, but I decide that I will first undertake a nostalgic pilgrimage through this beloved neighborhood. In pleasure & pain I gaze at the houses, sobbing & weeping in the street. Turning left (south) on S. Farmer Avenue, I am appalled to see that the houses on both sides of the street have been demolished & in their place a tacky, phoney "western town" has been constructed, modern housing for young slick, upper-middle class professionals. In grief, I walk to the site of our old Farmer Avenue apartments, search amid the wreckage there for some memento —a stone, a handful of earth – that I can take away with me.

8 Mar 90: I stand at the intersection of 10th Street & S. Farmer Avenue, just a few steps west of the r.r. tracks. I feel so very happy to be exactly where I am, doing just what I am doing, that I lean against a stop sign & weep with joy. The only thing that could make this moment more perfect than it now is would be the passage of a freight train.

28 Mar 90: I turn the key in the door of our old apartment at 1214 and a half S. Farmer Avenue. I open the door & encounter faces of surprise. These are the current occupants of the apartment. I don't live here anymore. I'm embarrassed but then remember that I live at 1218 S. Farmer, no. 3. I stand in front of the Judd House at 1208 S. Farmer looking at the one remaining palm tree there.

6 May 90: At dusk, I ride a bicycle west on 10th Street west of Mill Avenue, turn right on S. Farmer Avenue to see the old Farmer-Goodwin House at 820 S. Farmer Avenue with its overgrown garden.

12 May 90: Being driven in a car eastward along 13th Street. As we approach the intersection of 13th & S. Farmer Avenue, I see with sorrow & fury that the tall old Tamarisk tree that stood at the s.w. corner of the intersection has been felled, every trace of it removed! This sad sight provokes in me a raging rave of some minutes duration. My companion then inquires of me whether this means that Tempe is now completely devoid of attraction to me. Oh no, I reply, many worthwhile things yet remain.

21 May 90: We visit our former next door neighbor at 1218 S. Farmer Avenue who now occupies a flat that we once occupied at 1214 S. Farmer. I envy him all the years that he has lived in Tempe. From all about me, from every direction, I feel the pull, the tug, the attraction of Tempe.

23 May 90: We stand on the site of the apartments that formerly stood at 1214 & 1218 S. Farmer Avenue. Of the houses & buildings there, only a hole remains. Everything has been razed. I climb into the low hole, hoping to sift among the dirt for a piece of brick to save as a memento. The wonderful old Judd house at 1208 S. Farmer Avenue has also been levelled & in the distance I can see construction cranes where new faceless, graceless apartment buildings are being raised.

24 May 90: Walking with companions north on east side of Maple Avenue between 10th Street & University Drive. I point to the kind of houses that I find so attractive in this area (ever under threat from developers.) As we come to University Drive, I gesture across the street to the former site of Rundle's which has been demolished. In its stead, a multi-story building is under construction.

6 Jun 90: We wander the streets of the Maple/Ash district, yearning to live there.

5 Aug 90: We stand on the grounds just south of the apartments at 1218 S. Farmer Avenue. I sigh with longing to see the backyard of the house

just west across the alley (a Wilson Avenue address.) I note the tall radio antenna there still wound around with a string of Christmas lights. Walking east now to the sidewalk on Farmer, I gesture across the street to the little wooden houses there. "This," I say, "is where I would like to live."

18 Oct 90: Driven east in a car on Broadway Road. We turn left (north) onto S. Farmer Avenue, pass the ranch-style suburban houses there. Now, we cross 13th Street & I am delighted & deeply moved to see that the houses I so admire there are still intact, including the wonderful old wooden Judd house. I remark to the driver that I have so often dreamed of these streets & houses & in my dreams I have wept to be there. And now, as we proceed along S. Farmer to 10th Street, I weep & weep & feel at the same time joyful anticipation of the buildings & streets that we will soon see.

29 Oct 90: I take a cab to an area east of Mill Avenue & between the butte & University Drive. I'm seeking remnants of the past, remembering the old water-pump building that once stood near the s.e. corner of College Avenue & University Drive. I enter the office of the Mayor of Tempe who has instigated & presided over the destruction of old Tempe. He is dressed in tattered & threadbare longjohns. I strike his face again & again & as I do so repeat: "you are the man who ruined Tempe, you are the man who ruined Tempe." I want to force him to recognize the magnitude & gravity of his crimes.

30 Nov 90: I'm walking west in warm sunlight along the north side of 10th Street, at Ash Avenue. I look with close attention & keen appreciation at the houses on both sides of the street & I feel joy welling within me.

15 Jan 91: I stand looking at Pete's Fish & Chips on Mill Avenue between University Drive & 9th Street. I recall how long ago, *The New Times* had their offices nearby. And looking west, across the alley, I can see "the hovel" where we once lived (back house at 821 and a half S. Maple

Avenue.) Sitting at a table in Pete's Fish & Chips with a group of young students, I rant & fume about the folly of the Tempe City Council in demolishing the authentic old territorial buildings & replacing them with ersatz "Western style" buildings. And now I learn that the very building in which we are sitting is slated to be demolished. Indeed, this is the last day of existence for the venerable Pete's Fish & Chips.

14 Feb 91: It is early morning, just after dawn, & I stand on the sidewalk gazing at 1214 S. Farmer Avenue. To the west, I see a tall palm tree touched by the morning sun. I feel so happy, so exultant & triumphant just to be standing here. I gaze with pleasure at the dear Judd house & its one remaining palm tree & then take in the view north along Farmer toward distant mountains & Governor Hunt's white pyramid tomb. I picture in imagination the pleasant walks we could take here.

6 Mar 91: Living at 126 E. 6th Street. A guest calls upon us & I accompany him into the street, walking Forest Avenue to 5th Street. I recount to him the recent destruction of historic buildings & neighborhoods in Tempe, but I also remark that I yearned so intensely & for so many years to return to Tempe & now that I am here again I hope never again to leave.

14 Apr 91: Fascinated & gratified, I wander the streets between University Drive & 13th Street, between Mill Avenue & S. Farmer Avenue. I fear, however, that all will be destroyed by the relentless advance of blank-faced banality.

20 Apr 91: Driven in a friend's car west on 7th Street, we turn right at Mill Avenue. I'm very anxious to ascertain the state of the old buildings along Mill Avenue. How many & which have been demolished? I comment to my companion how fiercely I despise those persons responsible for the unconscionable, unforgivable ruin of Tempe.

6 May 91: I'm walking west on north side of 10th Street, just past Ash Avenue when I see an old couple sunning themselves on the grass there. I pause to chat with them & learn that they are the owners of the house

on the s.e. corner of 10th Street & S. Farmer Avenue, a little green house that I have always admired. Indeed, it is one of the houses in Tempe that I would most like to own.

30 May 91: I enter the Language & Literature building on the ASU campus, passing students & teachers entering & exiting. I am looking for the English Office in order to fill-out a job application. I feel sorrow & resentment at being an outsider here. Why can't I have a job here? How in the hell did these other teachers I see walking so confidently & purposefully in the corridors get to work here?

10 Jun 91: I roam the alley that runs from 13th tp 12th Street, between Wilson Avenue & S. Farmer Avenue, taking in every detail: the stones, the fences, the telephone poles, the backyards & sheds. I am "mystically connected to all this ... drawn by powerful & vivid longings & sympathies." (S. Bellow) In tears, I approach & touch a palo verde tree & silently ask it to pray for me.

13 Jun 91: I wander the streets of a part of Tempe previously unknown to me, an old quarter of mysterious Victorian houses with overgrown gardens. I hope these houses are not slated to be destroyed. I am aware that everything of interest in Tempe is ever at risk from developers.

22 Jun 91: I stand on S. Farmer Avenue about midway between University Drive & 13th Street. As far as I can see in either direction, on both sides of street, the houses have been razed. The only exceptions are two of the oldest houses which have been spared & will be "restored." I feel fury & despair.

17 Sep 91: We visit Tempe & survey the damage done by "urban renewal" & developers on Mill Avenue. Rundle's market has been torn down & a skyscraper is to be erected there.

30 Sep 91: Boxes of canned goods have been buried in an alley behind Tempe Center. With a confederate I retrieve the boxes & suggest that

we drive west on 10th Street to S. Farmer Avenue. I gaze with longing at the houses, their porches & trellises. "Oh, why can't I live here?" I exclaim in sorrow & frustration. My grief is compounded as I sense the strange, strong attraction of the surrounding streets.

17 Oct 91: I am reading a book about Tempe that causes me to feel almost giddy with rapture. Then I am walking in the alley that runs from University Drive to 13th Street, east of S. Maple Avenue & west of Mill Avenue. I am aware of the age of the earth beneath my feet, the long histories both human & geological.

31 Oct 91: Walking south on the west side of Ash Avenue between University Drive & 13th Street. I cherish each house I see & wish passionately I could live in one of them. I weep with joy to be here.

15 Nov 91: It's night & I sigh in my heart to see in the distance the Mill Avenue bridge. I walk from somewhere west of Mill Avenue to 3rd Street & Roosevelt. And now I am driven by a sheriff (just as a courtesy) past attractive houses & interesting shops & across the bridge to the north bank of the dry Salt River.

27 Nov 91: We return to Tempe & rent a house on S. Farmer Avenue across the street from the Judd house at 1208 S. Farmer, which I regard with deep affection. To my great satisfaction the trains run along the r.r. tracks just beyond the back gate of the house we're renting.

29 Nov 91: Walking with companions south on the east side of Ash Avenue, just south of University Drive. As we pass 821 S. Maple, behind which lies "the hovel" where we lived for a time, I am overcome with emotion & begin to weep. My companions are amazed by this display. I remark to them that I have often dreamed of old Tempe & in my dreams often wept to be there. Now we turn left (east) on 10th Street & cross Mill Avenue. As we approach the ASU campus, I exclaim: "Oh, why can't I get a job here?"

11 Jan 92: I dream that I am asleep dreaming of Tempe. In the dream within the dream I am weeping & repeating "Tempe, Tempe."

14 Jan 92: On the west side of Mill Avenue at 5th Street. Choking with emotion, I pray silently: "Oh God, please let me live here!"

3 Feb 92: Walking south on the west side Roosevelt Avenue in the direction of Broadway Road, considering that I could inquire at Jacques Cattell Press to see if I could work there again as a proofreader. I wonder if they would remember me now. And now I'm walking S. Farmer Avenue just north of Broadway, admiring houses & full grown trees. It would be so good to live here, I reflect, but there is not much possibility of my ever being able to afford a house here. Indeed, it is doubtful that I will ever find a job in Tempe.

13 Feb 92: A temporary stay in Tempe but I so keenly want to remain here. I walk on the west side of Ash Avenue northward from 13th Street. The houses enchant me, draw me. Oh, how I want to live here. I could walk this way, see these houses every day.

18 Mar 92: Walking north on the east side of S. Farmer Avenue, looking wistfully at the houses & apartments, weeping with longing to live here.

7 May 92: Being driven from Phoenix to Tempe. I tell the driver of my deep attraction to that particular place on the earth.

16 May 92: Ride a bus north on Mill Avenue, past the Grady Gammage auditorium. Then, sitting on a bench near the fountain on Orange Mall, ASU campus. I feel again that keen & tearful yearning to remain here.

26 May 92: I can buy the entire city of Tempe! I calculate the price, converting currencies. Yes, it's true, I can purchase the whole of the city & the surrounding area!

11 Jun 92: It's a warm summer night in Tempe. I walk south on the west side of Mill Avenue, past 13th Street. How lovely a night it is!

8 Nov 92: I'm walking north on the east side of Mill Avenue at 4th Street. It is so poignant to be once again in Tempe. And now I cross Mill Avenue & enter the Changing Hands bookstore.

3 Dec 92: Walking east on 7th Street east of Mill Avenue. I'm saddened to see that the houses have been replaced by bland modern apartment blocks. The whole quarter has been shorn of character & individuality.

13 Jan 93: We live in an apartment near the foot of Tempe Butte, at about 2nd Street.

19 Jan 93: Walking north on S. Farmer Avenue we cross 13th Street. I sigh & weep to see it all. Visit the apartments at 1218 & 1214 S. Farmer Ave & in sudden desperate determination, I cling with all my strength to the steel post supporting the porch in front of our old apartment. I will not let go. I will refuse to budge from here.

23 Jan 93: We have rented an apartment at 1218 S. Farmer Avenue. I feel fulfilled & happy to have returned.

9 Feb 93: In a real estate office on Mill Avenue (west side of the street, near 4th Street) we are negotiating for an apartment. We agree to wait in an adjacent room while inquiries are made, but hours pass & I despair. It is clear that we are being neglected, ignored.

11 Feb 93: Walking the alley that runs from 13th to 12th Street, between S. Farmer Avenue & S. Wilson Street, admiring the backyards. And now walking on Farmer I am pleased to see that the wonderful Judd house is still there. I exult to be here. I never wished anything more than just to walk down Farmer, taking pleasure in looking at the houses on both sides of the street.

24 Feb 93: Standing near the n.w. corner of Mill Avenue & University Drive. I am very eager to walk 10th Street, to see again the streets I love.

3 Mar 93: Houses are being razed along 13th Street between Mill Avenue & S. Wilson Street.

5 Mar 93: Walking on the west side of Mill Avenue, crossing 4th Street. I remark to a companion that I have never been able to envision a happy life residing anywhere other than in Tempe.

22 Mar 93: Walking north on Myrtle Avenue between University Drive & 10th Street. Now that I am here again I am determined to remain here.

30 Mar 93: Industrial Park Avenue. Even this most unprepossessing part of Tempe is not without interest. The bakery where I used to buy day-old bread is still there.

22 May 93: Walking north through the alley that runs from 13th Street to 12th Street, between S. Farmer Avenue & S. Wilson Street. Passing that patch of ground where long ago I tried to raise carrots, I am swept with nostalgia.

25 Jun 93: Strolling in satisfaction & contentment northward on the west side of Mill Avenue between 13th & University Drive. How happy I am to be here & to have the downtown shops in which to browse. We live in an apartment on the west side of Ash Avenue near 10th Street.

7 Jul 93: Heading south on a bus, moving along Ash Avenue between 10th & 13th Streets. I am so intensely attracted to the houses I see that I am having difficulty in repressing my tears & sobs from the other passengers. And now we turn right (west) on 13th Street & pass the alley of dear memory.

13 Jul 93: The wonder & mystery of Tempe: walk S. Farmer Avenue near 13th Street. And now it is night. Walk the stony alley, passing behind our old apartments.

23 Jul 93: We are renting one of the little wooden cabins at the 1920s wooden motorcourt at 2nd Street & Ash Avenue.

25 Jul 93: I'm standing on the south bank of the Salt River near the old Ash Avenue bridge. Due to heavy rains in the north of the state, the Salt River is flowing. The current is swift & I watch as the river sweeps past the old bridge.

7 Aug 93: Carefully arranging the lids of trash bins in the alley behind the apartments at 1214 & 1218 S. Farmer Ave. Walking past the open door & windows of our old apartment, I remark to a companion how fiercely & dearly I would like to live there again.

6 Sep 93: All night in Tempe there has been a storm: lightning, thunder, wind, hard rain. Now, just before dawn, all is calm & I anticipate with joy a long walk through the fertile, fascinating streets of the city.

28 Sep 93: With companions, I walk north on Wilson Avenue, north of 13th Street. I gaze with amazement & pleasure at the houses. Then, overwhelmed, I throw myself to the ground, wailing "I can't bear it! I can't take it!" I feel so unbearably tantalized, so tormented with yearning.

3 Oct 93: The streets & houses of Tempe. Rich & resonant, fecund, intriguing, drawing me.

24 Nov 93: Between 4th & 5th Streets, west of Mill Avenue. The houses & buildings here have not yet been destroyed. An aura of mystery & quirky grace still linger in these streets.

12 Dec 93: Walking west on north side of 10th Street, just past Maple Avenue. Exhilarated to be here.

24 Dec 93: 7th Street just east of Myrtle Avenue. Tears of self-pity fall from my eyes as I complain to a companion that all I have ever desired in my life was to live a modest & simple life in Tempe, walking to work every morning.

28 Dec 93: I'm riding into Tempe on the hood of a Volkswagen, clinging for safety to handholds. We turn left from Broadway Road onto Mill Avenue, pass Tempe High School on our left. Banal & soulless new buildings but soon (we're approaching 10th Street) we will see the old good things.

12 Jan 94: I exult & feel exalted to be walking east on the north side of 10th Street at Ash Avenue.

24 Jan 94: Sitting with companions at a table in the grassy sideyard of the little house on the s.e. corner of 10th Street & S. Farmer Avenue. I have planned a walk for us all: north on Farmer to University Drive, turn right on Ash Avenue & walk the blocks to 13th Street, turn left there & left on Maple Avenue, walking the length of that street back to University Drive. As we begin our walk on Farmer, I remark to my companions how very strange it is for me to be here & to be doing this as I have dreamed of this area so many times for so many years.

28 Jan 94: Walk east side of Mill Avenue from 6th Street to Tempe Bridge.

18 Feb 94: The weather is mild & it is a pleasure for me to walk the streets of Tempe. This fertile quarter of the city (west of Mill Avenue, from 2nd to 5th Streets, as far west as Roosevelt Avenue) intrigues & stimulates me.

17 Mar 94: As evening falls, I walk the Maple/Ash/Farmer quarter. The evening air is soft & warm, the light is fading. I weep with joy to be there.

We have returned to Tempe & it is our first morning there. I feel keenest excitement at the prospect of exploring the city. We stand on Myrtle Avenue at 7th Street, delighted to recognize old houses & landmarks (including the American Indian Crafts store on the n.w. corner of 7th & Myrtle & the First Congregational Church on the s.e. corner of Myrtle & 6th.) Ah, now I see the old Russian olive tree whose fallen olives used to stain the concrete sidewalk. I weep to see it all again.

15 Apr 94: Standing at the intersection of 13th Street & S. Farmer Avenue. I walk west on the north side of 13th because – for sentimental reasons – I want to see the boat beached in a backyard that I used to see every afternoon when I walked home from my proofreading job at Jacque Cattell Press. I look around at the houses, streets & alleys, feeling awe & happiness. Soon, I will walk S. Farmer to 10th Street. I'm on the verge of tears.

18 Apr 94: It's night & I walk with companions in that mysterious old n.w. quarter of Tempe (bounded by Roosevelt to w., Mill Avenue to e., encompassing 2nd to 5th Streets.) I pause to listen to the crickets singing. It's wonderful to hear them chirping in the warm darkness. I lead my companions to the porch of an old house with a long, narrow porch supported by wooden posts. The house dates from territorial days & I feel the mystery of all the lives of those who have inhabited this dwelling, those who looked out the windows in past years.

18 May 94: Walking the alley that runs between University Drive & 10th Street, between Mill Avenue & S. Maple Street. I stop to examine some bushes that have blossomed, admiring their beauty. I feel uplifted & happy.

2 Jun 94: I am walking west on the north side of 13th Street, at Wilson Avenue. I have just returned to Tempe & I want to see if that boat is still there in a backyard. In my long years of absence from Tempe I have often remembered that boat. I see it! I exclaim & feel that painful joy of having really, truly returned to Tempe.

12 Jun 94: Walking south on the west side of Mill Avenue between 10th & 13th Streets, remembering long ago walks here, taking pleasure in all that I see & all that I anticipate seeing. I intend to turn right (west) on 13th & walk to S. Farmer Avenue, then turn right (north) & walk to 10th Street.

7 Jul 94: Browsing in a large library, I come upon a book of photographs taken in the south-western United States. Hoping to find a photo of Tempe, I sit at a table & turn the pages of the book. There is an aerial view of the city! I recognize Old Main, St. Mary's church, Campus Drugs, Tempe Center, Tempe Butte & more. I sigh to see these things & wonder if perhaps I were myself somewhere in Tempe on the day on which the photograph was taken.

15 Jul 94: We have just returned to live in Tempe & are renting an apartment at 1218 S. Farmer Avenue. We walk westward on 13th, past the alley, to Wilson Avenue. I feel pleasant anticipation at the prospect of walking north on Wilson.

19 Aug 94: Riding a bus on Apache Road, I look eagerly & attentively out of the window. I am looking forward to when the bus stops on College Avenue near St. Mary's church.

1 Sep 94: I stand looking at the Farmer-Goodwin house at 820 S. Farmer Avenue. I remember when it was shabby & unkempt & you could rent an apartment there. Now the house & grounds have been spiffed up. There is a man working in the front yard & I inquire as to a possible rental apartment there. There will be a vacancy in the fall, he informs me. The possibility of living there is very attractive to me.

25 Sep 94: With a companion, I walk east along the north side of University Drive, east of Forest Avenue. We come upon an old house currently occupied by a shop. We mount the wooden stairs, admire the porch with its round pillars. We enter & regard with pleasure & interest the old linoleum floor.

2 Oct 94: Walking east on the north side of 10th Street at Ash Avenue. Looking to my left (north) I see with sorrow that nearly all of the houses on both sides of Ash have been levelled. Only a few splintered stumps of trees remain to indicate that there was once a neighbourhood here.

8 Oct 94: I'm walking north on Mill Avenue from E. Southern Avenue. I remember having walked this way once long ago. Now, to the west I hear the rumble of a freight train & then I see the train moving north. A stirring sight!

6 Nov 94: I'm here! The enchantment, the magic, the magnetic attraction of Tempe.

14 Nov 94: Walking with a companion along the south bank of the dry bed of the Salt River, east of Tempe Bridge. I intend to walk the area on the west side of the bridge, then Mill Avenue. To my companion, I remark that I believe it is my destiny to live here in Tempe. I feel as if the city itself, this place, like a sentient entity, will guide me.

18 Nov 94: Browsing in a bookshop on the west side of S. Forest Avenue, between 7th Street & University Drive. I enjoy this & it is thrilling to be in Tempe.

27 Nov 94: We have just moved back into an apartment at 1218 S. Farmer Avenue. I'm standing on the sidewalk when a large yellow bull-dozer pulls up & the driver inquires of me if I know where Wilson Street is. I give him instructions, pointing the way, but then fear that he may be on his way to raze houses to make way for "robot apartments." Now, I

turn & regard the houses behind me. A rush of happiness lifts my spirit. I am so very glad to be here.

13 Dec 94: Chatting amiably with others in the manager's office above the lobby of the Valley Art Theatre. I inspect some wooden shelves along one wall & note an old time usher's hat displayed there. I wonder what became of Bill Grieg, the projectionist here at the Valley Art? And now the film is about to begin. Together with other eager customers, I enter the seating area. I gaze in gladness at the walls & roof, the lamps & screen, remarking to my companion that I have longed & yearned for so many years to be here again, wondering if I would ever again sit in the dear Valley Art Theatre.

21 Dec 94: I'm riding a bus north along Wilson Avenue south of University Drive. The bus turns onto University & I expect it to turn left onto Mill Avenue, but instead it continues east on University, stopping near St. Mary's church. I will walk back to Mill Avenue. As I glance around me, I am struck with that sense of mystery, that thrill of pleasure & attraction that I have so often felt in Tempe. Everything I see seems interesting & appealing to me. Oh, I want to move to Tempe NOW. But I don't believe that it would be economically feasible. I must have a job.

27 Dec 94: I'm jogging west along the sidewalk on the north side of 13th Street, turn left (south) on Roosevelt, running toward Clark Park. I am aware that I used to run this route on blazing hot afternoons long ago. And now I am on S. Farmer Avenue just north of 13th, remarking to my companion how much I love Tempe. I have an appointment for a job interview.

13 Jan 95: I walk south on S. Farmer Avenue (near 9th) on the west side of the street. I pause to study the Farmer-Goodwin house with its untended, overgrown garden that I explored long ago. Now, I'm standing at the old Tempe train depot at 3rd Street & Ash Avenue, admiring a couple of flat cars & gondolas. And now I'm walking on the

west side of Mill Avenue, at 7th Street. It is a calm, vast afternoon. The sunlight is soft.

20 Jan 95: Walking south through the alley that runs between 13th & 12th Streets, between Wilson & Farmer. I note the spot where once we tended a garden, including some marijuana plants.

2 Feb 95: We have returned to live in Tempe & have been invited to dinner in a spacious, old house on Maple Avenue between 10th & 13th Streets. A large spliff is passed around & I tell of my long-standing yearning to return to Tempe.

4 Feb 95: I turn left at the corner of Roosevelt & 13th Street, walk east on my way to S. Farmer Avenue. Glad to be there, feeling a deep affinity with this place.

7 Feb 95: In conversation, mention is made of a professor who taught at ASU. I remember that he used to live in a modest apartment on 13th Street between S. Farmer Avenue & Ash Avenue. Immediately, in my soul I feel a sharp pang & exclaim: "Oh, I wish that I were there now!"

19 Mar 95: Walking east on the north side of E. 6th Street, between Mill Avenue & Myrtle Avenue. With wonder & delight I realize that somehow after all the many years of yearning, I have at long, long last returned to live in Tempe.

6 Apr 95: I stand at 10th Street & S. Farmer Avenue, facing west. I'm relieved to see that the neighborhood immediately before me remains largely intact & unchanged. But in the distance, to the west, on Wilson, a high rise building looms. I think with dismay of the many charming houses that this Molochian monstrosity has displaced.

9 May 95: We are approaching Tempe Bridge! Driven by a friend, I cross the bridge onto Mill Avenue. I can hardly bear the excitement I feel.

Now I will be able to visit the streets of my dreams. I'm actually here & I'm really going to see it all!

17 May 95: With careful attention I browse the shelves at Changing Hands Bookstore on Mill Avenue. This is a pleasure.

11 Jun 95: At my request, a friend has driven me to Tempe & we are travelling south on Ash Avenue north of University Drive. I am exhilarated to see before me the Tempe I have so longed to see. I roll down the car window & shout: "I love this place!" I have booked a room at the Travel Lodge motel on the s.w. corner of 9th Street & Mill Avenue. I feel intense excitement at the prospect of walking the streets of Tempe.

5 Aug 95: With a companion, walking west on the north side of 10th Street. I look right & left (north & south) along Ash Avenue as we pass it & I feel the force field of its mystery. And, now as we cross the r.r. tracks & step onto S. Farmer Avenue, I gaze with deep satisfaction at the houses & foliage. I gesture & exclaim to my companion: "This is the very place on earth that I love best of all!"

6 Aug 95: I am eager to undertake my pilgrimage through the streets of Tempe but it is raining hard. Soon, though, I will view the dear & familiar streets.

10 Aug 95: From a distance, I suddenly see Tempe. I begin to walk toward it.

9 Sep 95: A friend has sent me a hologram photo of Tempe; a view of Mill Avenue. And now we are there. I'm relieved & pleased to see that the street is still rather attractive, with interesting shops & bars. Later, we walk 6th Street & Ash Avenue. Eagerly & carefully, I study each house, taking intense pleasure in seeing them. Occupants of one old wooden house are engaged in painting the outside walls. I am nearly delirious with the allure of the house, falling to the grass in the sideyard

& weeping. My astonished companion asks to know the cause of my distress. "It's because I've been gone for so many years," I reply. We pass another old house & I continue to weep. In tears, I address my companion: "This is all I have ever wanted."

23 Sep 95: Full of glee, I rush to our old apartment at 1214 S. Farmer Avenue, which we have succeeded in renting again. There are the oleander bushes & there is the porch & the door. It is a keen pleasure to think that tomorrow we will awaken again here in these rooms.

4 Oct 95: I have 24 hours in Tempe. I will re-visit the streets & places dear to me.

8 Oct 95: Rapturous & vividly alive, I walk Ash Avenue to 10th Street, turn right (west) toward S. Farmer Avenue. I take in every detail of what is before my eyes.

26 Oct 95: A friend has rented our old apartment at 1214 S. Farmer Avenue. We sit upstairs talking & my friend relates a tale of how as a frail old man a famous bandit of the late frontier era once lived here.

2 Nov 95: A brief stay in Tempe. I stand on Mill Avenue, feeling fond attraction & glad anticipation. I look around at the shops & the Valley Art Theatre. "Oh, why can't I live here?" I exclaim.

13 Nov 95: Silently, I give thanks to God that I have returned to live at 1218 S. Farmer Avenue. I note that in the backyard there is a bare patch of earth. I can plant a small garden there.

16 Nov 95: Ascending in an elevator in the Hayden Library at ASU. How very gratified I am to be able to pursue my research in this fine library. Others cannot imagine how exciting & stimulating a good library is.

29 Nov 95: It's dusk & I have just arrived in Tempe for a visit. I stand regarding with pleasure & envy the Judd house at 1208 S. Farmer

Avenue. And now, standing at 10th Street & Farmer, with joy & wonder I devour with my eyes the sights around me. The light is fading but still I stare entranced at the houses on Ash Avenue, the porches, the lamplit front rooms. "Oh, I want to live here!" I cry.

I'm walking 10th Street east of Mill Avenue at Myrtle Avenue, making my way to the ASU campus. I cross Forest Avenue & walk toward the fountain on Orange Mall. I am euphoric. Soon I will pass the Moeur Administration Building & I will see the fountain. I have long dreamed of such a moment.

16 Dec 95: Walking on the east side of Mill Avenue, approaching the former site of the Laird & Dines Drugstore, currently occupied by a shop selling tawdry, corny merchandise.

10 Jan 96: Walking with a companion on S. Farmer Avenue at 10th Street. I am eager to show him the particulars & details of the houses here. I feel excitement & elation & visceral attraction.

3 Feb 96: I have temporarily rented an apartment at 1218 S. Farmer Avenue & have invited an old couple who live nearby to dine with me. We walk from their house – near 13th Street – in the red light of dusk. I can hear the whooping cries of the mockingbirds perched in the trees. As we enter my apartment, I begin to weep. "I so want to stay here," I say, "I don't want to leave." Tears course down my face.

Walking south on the west side of Maple Avenue at 9th Street, feeling once again that profound attraction to these streets. On 10th Street, I turn right & walk in the direction of S. Farmer Avenue. I weep, passionately wishing I could remain here.

8 Feb 96: The west side of Myrtle Avenue between 6th & 7th Streets & then through the alley that runs between S. Forest Avenue & S. College Avenue. Backyards, rear entrances to buildings. All that I have seen is so

interesting & evokes in my body a thrill of excitement. I run into Professor Nicholas Salerno & we talk at length of my situation.

16 Feb 96: Deeply attracted to the streets & sidewalks & houses of S. Farmer Avenue. A mysterious kinship, a deep rapport.

Fertile, mysterious sidestreets of the Maple/Ash neighbourhood. Looking for a rental apartment. Bewilderment, aggrievement. To a companion, I remark: "Why can't I live here?"

20 Feb 96: We pull up in a car to the curb in front of 1218 S. Farmer Avenue. I hope to find a rental apartment here.

7 Mar 96: Visiting the present occupants of our old apartment at 1214 and a half S. Farmer Avenue, No. 1.

10 Mar 96: Returned to Tempe & living happily in an apartment there.

12 Mar 96: Talking to resident of apartment at 1214 S. Farmer Avenue. He informs me that the city council has plans for the destruction of everything between Mill Avenue & Roosevelt & between University &

13th Street. The whole of the district I so love will be demolished to make way for "commercial development." I vent my spleen in a long string of curses & imprecations.

15 Mar 96: Walking north along the sidewalk that runs in front of the shops at Tempe Center. Just passing the windows of "Books, Etc." Dusk is gathering, birds are singing their lilting, musical whistles & warbles. I am swept with amazement & excitement, moved to wonder. I am actually here in Tempe.

19 Mar 96: Standing in front of the Farmer-Goodwin house at 820 S. Farmer Avenue. I'm stroking & talking to a cat that perches outside the

house. I can hear the swish of traffic passing on University Drive & the rumble of a train approaching. I feel keen excitement & deep attraction.

4 Apr 96: A former workmate from Datagraphics gives me a lift in his Volksvagen van from Mill Avenue to 10th Street. We turn right (west) & passing Maple & Ash, I feel a thrill of joy & the powerful pull of the place. And now, as cars & bicycles pass us, we sit eating a picnic lunch on the r.r. tracks at 10th Street & S. Farmer Avenue.

25 Apr 96: I am in the office of the Tempe Daily News, fulminating to an editor there over the destruction of the old territorial buildings & adjacent neighborhoods. Nearly everything has been lost, I tell him.

2 May 96: In "Books, Etc" at Tempe Center, I find a first edition of Jack Kerouac's *Book of Dreams*. (Found in a dream!)

10 May 96: Living again in Tempe. I realize that I have forgotten to register to vote.

17 Jun 96: On 3rd Street west of Mill Avenue. I can see that there are still some attractive old apartments here with quirky features (such as a brightly painted birdhouse high atop a pole in a front yard.) It would be an adventure to find a place to live in this old quarter so near the dry Salt River bed.

21 Jul 96: In dim, gray pre-dawn light, we stand on the n.w. corner of 10th Street & Mill Avenue. We have returned & it is our intention to stay in Tempe. I feel excited, elated, optimistic, animated by a sense of potentials & possibilities. We begin to walk west on 10th Street. I pick up a broom that has been cast away & as we walk I begin to sweep the street with it. The street is still wet with dew & I can see the light of the streetlamps reflected there. As we approach 10th & Ash, I am so deeply moved that I weep & exclaim: "I never thought I'd ever get back again, I never thought I'd ever get back again!"

23 Jul 96: On a brief visit to Tempe. I have just bought some item at the convenience store (Circle K or 7-11) at the corner of Broadway Road & Roosevelt Avenue. I look about me & note the insipid architecture, the vacuous, inert ambiance here. Now, I will walk north to 13th & then to S. Farmer Avenue. I resolve to note and commit to memory every detail of what I see.

27 Jul 96: How deeply pleased, how glad & satisfied I feel to be living again at 1218 S. Farmer Avenue. I feel sympathetic communion with all that I behold: the white water heaters, the trash bins, the weeds growing in the alley, the cacti, the telephone poles, the tall palm trees & oleander bushes. This is what I have wished for so ardently & for so long a time.

15 Aug 96: Walking south on west side of Ash Avenue between 10th & 13th Streets. I'm on the verge of tears, wishing desperately that we could live in one of these handsome old houses that I see.

16 Aug 96: I wake in a house on Ash Avenue near 13th Street. I walk south on Ash to 13th, enraptured & elevated to be where I am & to see what I am seeing. I scrutinize every detail in my field of sight: the sidewalk, the cracked black asphalt pavement, the blades of grass, the white feathery clouds in the blue sky above me.

26 Aug 96: I hear a train approaching along the r.r. tracks from the south & I run to 13th Street where I will have a clear view as it passes. Yes, there is the engine! I wave to the engineer who returns my wave. This is a pleasure! And I'm so glad to be here.

3 Sep 96: S. Farmer Avenue just south of 10th Street.

Walking west on north side of 10th below Mill Avenue in the direction of S. Farmer Avenue.

It's dusk. I'm walking on the west side of Ash Avenue between 9th & 10th Streets. Ah, the handsome old houses!

Standing in the alley that runs between 13th & 12th Streets, between S. Farmer Avenue & Wilson Avenue. Adjusting a wooden trellis.

9 Sep 96: Walking west on University Drive, between S. Farmer Avenue & Wilson Avenue. I am stirred to see a number of fine old houses.

12 Sep 96: We are in the backyard of 1222 S. Farmer Avenue.

17 Sep 96: Walking the alleys of the old Maple/Ash/Farmer neighborhood. I remark to a companion how much I like alleys.

30 Sep 96: Looking for an apartment to rent at our former address on S. Farmer Avenue. Later, walking ASU campus. And, then, 10th Street & Myrtle Avenue with its long sidewalk stained with fallen olives.

8 Oct 96: Night in Tempe, walking the streets under wonderful starry skies: south of 13th Street between Maple & Wilson. Soon, I will walk north to S. Farmer Avenue.

4 Nov 96: We have only a few hours to undertake a visit to Tempe. We walk south on the east side of Maple Avenue, south of University Drive. Cosy, desirable bungalows. I feel animated, uplifted, aware of the surrounding streets, their houses, yards, trees & sidewalks. And then, there are the r.r. tracks!

29 Nov 96: Walking north on the west side of S. Farmer Avenue, from 13th Street toward 10th Street. I examine carefully each house, every architectural detail. To my left, on W. 11th Street, I see a rental sign for half a duplex. The tenant who is moving out emerges from the door to dispose of some trash. I inquire as to the rent & learn that it is 125 dollars a month, though she is also obliged to do some gardening & minor upkeep. I'm very favorably impressed.

6 Dec 96: I am enraptured, disbelieving. We have returned to live in Tempe & found an apartment on Ash Avenue just south of 10th Street. As we walk the streets, I feel intoxicated by my good fortune.

14 Dec 96: Walking west on the north side of 10th Street. As I pass Maple Avenue on my right, I see a deer grazing in a vacant lot. An enchanting sight. Indeed, there is something altogether pastoral about this neighborhood.

17 Dec 96: We have rented our old apartment at 1218 S. Farmer Avenue & are preparing to spend our first night there – our first night within those walls & under that roof in many years.

24 Dec 96: In the final hour of a brief visit to Tempe, I take a bus north on Mill Avenue, across Tempe Bridge & into Papago Park. I climb a hill, stand atop a boulder, & below me in a kind of valley I see a young horse grazing.

28 Dec 96: A temporary return but at least I can spend a year in Tempe.

12 Jan 97: Walking north on the ASU campus, the Language & Literature building to my right. I want to find the strange old "Philomathian" bench that I came upon once long ago. Then, seeing it again after so many years, I feel profoundly moved, weep. It has been here all the years that I have been gone. Then, as we approach the rear entrance to the L. & L. building, I am again moved to tears. I desperately want to stay here.

19 Jan 97: Having returned to Tempe & rented an apartment at 1218 S. Farmer Avenue, I walk the alley exulting in my excellent good fortune. I look with appreciation & close attention at the scene before me: the way the sunlight slants on the wooden shed behind the Judd house, the texture of the old wood of which it is built, the flaking paint. I anticipate the many days ahead on which I can see how the moving sun turns the shadows of trees & telephone poles. And now, I have entered the Judd

house. I examine a framed engraving hanging on a wall & am amazed & fascinated to learn that on this site & the site next door there was once – in the late 19th & early 20th century – a boarding house run by Dutch immigrants.

24 Jan 97: Walking behind the Hayden Flour Mill, along the base of Tempe Butte. I'm navigating my route by sighting on the steeple of St. Mary's church. I think how I would like to use a trowel & dig here, perhaps finding in the earth some Indian or pioneer artefact.

Attentive, excited, admiring all that I see, I am walking south on the east side of Forest Avenue at 6th Street.

29 Jan 97: From the Hayden Library north to a student dormitory. I explain to a student my plight, my pain: I've written 5 books & have another one in progress but no job, no prospects.

30 Jan 97: The ASU campus, the Language & Literature building. I enter the glass doors & am struck with sorrow & a sense of hopelessness. I will never work here. It is my highest wish, my dearest dream to do so but it will never happen. Downcast, I ascend the stairs, walk the corridors, look into the open doors of classrooms.

13 Feb 97: Walking south on the east side of S. Farmer Avenue at 11th Street, heading toward the apartments at 1214 & 1218.

18 Feb 97: Having crossed Tempe Bridge, we are just north of the Salt River. Just an excursion, a bit of exploration, a micro adventure.

22 Feb 97: Living again in our former apartment at 1218 S. Farmer Avenue, no. 3. It's night & I stand in the alley just behind the apartments. The crickets are singing. I exult in my situation. To a companion, I remark: "You have no conception how glad I am to be here."

1 Mar 97: I am about to enter the Language & Literature building on the ASU campus. An old acquaintance stops me to inquire about an apartment rental: price, procedure etc.

30 Mar 97: Living again at 1218 S. Farmer Avenue (in the front apartment facing the street.) It is night. I walk back to the alley, then forward to the sidewalk of Farmer, gaze at the Judd house. How happy & contented I am! This is what I have longed for.

8 Apr 97: We visit our former apartments on S. Farmer Avenue. The flat at 1214 and a half, No. 1, has been gutted by fire. I stand in the place that was once our living room, my feet on charred wood, looking up at the broken, smoke-blackened windows.

14 Apr 97: I stand near r.r. tracks & realize that this is the line that crosses the Salt River over the old railroad bridge & passes through Tempe. Tempe is only a few miles away. I could walk the tracks & be there in less than an hour. The prospect pleases & uplifts me.

18 Apr 97: Returned to live at 1218 S. Farmer Avenue, no. 3. I am eager to inspect every detail of the immediate environment: the gas meters, the hot water heaters, the plants, the alley.

8 May 97: In the distance – yet somehow in vivid detail – I can see the apartments on S. Farmer Avenue. I determine to find a way to move in there.

14 May 97: Walking south on the east side of Ash Avenue north of University Drive. I remember walking this same route one winter's night, taking in the romance of old Tempe. Now, I am disheartened to see the destruction that has taken place along this street: handsome houses and old buildings demolished, slick, soulless apartment blocks in their place. I cross University & proceed along Ash, intrigued & attracted by a large two-story house that dates from frontier days.

4 Jun 97: Living again in apartment no. 3 at 1218 S. Farmer Avenue. I walk the alley.

6 June 97: In the gutter in front of 1214 S. Farmer Avenue, I find a pocket appointment book from 1910. It is handsomely bound in leather with colored flowers under glass on the front cover. There is a page for each day of the year & color reproductions of famous paintings, including – to my surprise – a painting by Georgio de Chirico.

2 Jul 97: Early morning on S. Farmer Avenue. I talk to an elderly man who opens & closes the irrigation valves for the city. Now, I walk among the apartments. I note that the door to no. 3 is open. I knock & explain to occupants that I once lived here. I am admitted, take note of the interior: the walls, the floor. Now, I collapse, weeping. I explain to the astonished occupants that I have long nourished a deep, intense attraction to Tempe and to this particular place, of which I have often dreamed. I wonder if they ever find any traces of the past? Any artefacts of former residents?

4 Jul 97: Walking from class in Language & Literature building on ASU campus south & west toward 10th Street. Across Mill Avenue (on the west side of the street) I note with approval a hollowed out palm tree that has been converted into a gazebo of sorts. This is the kind of bohemian ingenuity that has for me from the first been an attractive feature of Tempe.

9 Jul 97: Watching a late night screening of a foreign film at the Valley Art Theatre. From my seat in the dark, I inspect every aspect of the interior of the theatre: the ceiling, the lamps, the old carpet and bare floor, the metal backs of the folding cushioned seats, the wooden stage at the far end. And now, the film ended, the audience files out into the lobby. I saunter & explore the upstairs rooms & hallways. I even look through the open door of the projection booth & hope to talk with the projectionist, old Bill Grieg. At length, I re-enter the theatre, seating

myself for the next feature. I am aware of my long sentimental association with this cinema & am filled with delight to be here.

6 Aug 97: Walking on the west side of S. Farmer Avenue just south of University Drive. I am irate to see the inroads made by developers here but I rejoice to see that the neighborhood is still largely intact & it gives me much pleasure to be here again.

29 Sep 97: I visit the apartments at 1218 S. Farmer Avenue to make inquiries as to rent & to secure the name & phone number of the current owner or manager of the apartments. I am permitted by occupants to enter & view one apartment there (though it is not one hallowed by memories.) I tell the occupants of my long-standing, ardent desire to return to Tempe & to this very location. I explain that I have for many years had the conviction that I could never be happy anywhere else than here & cannot envision happiness without imagining myself living here.

27 Oct 97: I tell the owner of the properties at 1214 & 1218 S. Farmer Avenue of my profound, intense & enduring attraction to these apartments. Later, I walk the grounds & the alley with a resident of the apartments, telling him that I have dreamed again & again & again of doing just these things. I sigh with contentment.

11 Nov 97: It is night & having just returned to live in Tempe, we stand on the west side of Mill Avenue at 7th Street. I am stimulated, full of anticipation, but I grieve to see the new buildings that have replaced the original, authentic territorial buildings. Soon we will walk to Changing Hands Bookstore at 414 S. Mill Avenue. I look up at the night sky remembering other starry nights in Tempe.

23 Nov 97: Visiting the apartments at 1214 & 1218 S. Farmer Avenue. I'm inspecting some large stones placed near the oleander bushes for purposes of landscaping. I want to make some kind of marking on one of the stones, scratch my name or initials, engrave some kind of lasting mark so that when I am again far away from this place, even as time

passes, I can think of my mark here enduring the weathers & seasons. I also want to bury a coin in the earth here so that I will know that some trace of my presence remains here. The thought of having left something of myself in this place would somehow comfort me in time to be.

29 Dec 97: I'm walking west on the north side of 13th Street. At the corner of Ash & 13th, I am recognized by a postman who now delivers to me letters somehow undeliverable nearly 20 years ago. I proceed to the apartments at 1214 & 1218 S. Farmer Avenue. I contemplate with pleasure a long, leisurely, deliberate stroll through the streets of Tempe.

8 Jan 98: Short in stature, slick, self-satisfied, the mayor of Tempe addresses a reporter. The mayor boasts of the "rehabilitation" of the downtown, by which, of course, he means the destruction of block upon block of historic buildings & their replacement by a bland, banal & dismal cityscape. I see before me the deplorable results of his vaunted "rehabilitation" & weep with rage & sorrow.

17 Jan 98: We are making a brief nostalgic pilgrimage to our former apartment at 1218 S. Farmer Avenue, no. 3. We persuade the current residents there to permit us to enter. I gaze at the red carpeting on the floor, remembering the many times we sat here on cushions working, reading & talking.

19 Jan 98: While awaiting a vacancy among the apartments at 1214 & 1218 S. Farmer Avenue, I have installed myself in quarters nearby. The small shed in which I live is located in the alley that runs between 13th & 12th Streets. I speak to one of the current occupants of the apartments.

24 Jan 98: I watch from above (an aerial view) events that took place in Tempe more than a century ago. It is the shooting of Tom Graham. From a great height I see the fields & dirt roads south of Broadway Road. As Tom Graham is fired upon, I see the smoke from the discharged weapon, though I can't hear the report of the shot.

2 Feb 98: A leisurely walk west on the north side of 13th Street west of
Mill Avenue. I decide to turn right (north) on Ash Avenue to view the
houses there. The day is warm. I hear a pig grunting & see a lot between
two houses on Ash where horses & pigs are kept in a corral. I am acutely
interested in & powerfully attracted by all that I see.

8 Feb 98: I return to Tempe to seek work there. I have ridden a freight
train across the old r.r. bridge & into the city. (What a triumph!) I stand
now by the Casa Vieja. I must find work or I will have to return to
Europe.

9 Feb 98: Living in a boarding house on 10th Street. It is a large, old
house located on the south side of 10th Street between Maple & Ash. I've
only recently returned to Tempe.

21 Feb 98: We have found living quarters in those mysterious old adobe
buildings that stand hidden behind more modern buildings near the
n.w. corner of Mill Avenue & University Drive.

7 Mar 98: I'm staying temporarily in the Travel Lodge motel, located on
the s.w. corner of 9th Street & Mill Avenue

23 Mar 98: We are walking north in the alley that runs from 12th to 13th
Street, between S. Farmer Avenue & Wilson Avenue. I am enlivened &
uplifted just to see the backyard & the white water heaters behind the
apartments there. We view the door & window of our old apartment at
no. 3. Then, we walk to the apartments that front the street, where we
one evening we held "a roof party." Near the alley, I see with a pang the
dry plot of ground where I once tried to cultivate a garden. Oh, I want
so much to live here again! I crave & wish & want to live here.

30 Mar 98: I am again living in Tempe, working for the preservation of
the old territorial buildings. One of the old buildings is soon to be torn
down. It is the Casa Vieja! I am furious & saddened at this news. I wish I
could save even some fragment of that historic building, even a hinge or

metal key hole. But all will soon be destroyed. Not a trace will remain. The juggernaut of dullness rolls on, flattening all before it.

4 Apr 98: Riding in an automobile from Phoenix to Tempe. Soon we will be there. I will see it again. In silent happiness I know this.

22 Apr 98: So dense with meaning & memory, 1218 S. Farmer Avenue. Excited, eager I rush to see the apartments there.

3 Jun 98: My goal is an apartment where I currently reside on Ash Avenue near University Drive. I'm walking west on the north side of 13th Street, heading toward my apartment. Filled with pleasant anticipation, I turn right (north) on Maple Avenue. Each house invites my attention & excites my admiration. And now, a man & woman, walking south, pass me on my left. I overhear the young woman declare to her companion that the walk they have taken along Maple Avenue was "the best walk of my life." I continue my walk, stirred by the beauty of the houses.

9 Jul 98: With a companion, I visit 1218 S. Farmer Avenue. I recount how once in the backyard near the alley we grew tall marijuana plants which under cover of darkness were uprooted & stolen from us.

2 Aug 98: We are living in an apartment across the street from 1214 & 1218 S. Farmer Avenue, hoping ultimately to secure a rental in the apartments opposite us. I walk to the intersection of S. Farmer Avenue & 10th Street. I feel from the streets surrounding me the invisible but powerful pull, the mystery of the place drawing me.

13 Aug 98: I stand with a companion on the north side of Broadway Road across the busy street from S. Farmer Avenue to which we intend to cross. In the swift & constant traffic, it is difficult, but at length, we succeed in traversing the street.

22 Aug 98: Living again in apartment no. 3, 1218 S. Farmer Avenue.

10 Oct 98: In the alley that runs from 12th to 13th Street, between S. Farmer Avenue & Wilson Avenue, I find a pair of rusted animal (vaccination, registration) tags on a rusted chain. The engraved letters are nearly illegible but I can see that the date is July 6th, 1972. I read & recognize, too, the engraved name of the dog. It was a little dog that belonged to our friends & next door neighbors. The metal tags make a poignant artefact of that time.

22 Oct 98: With an old man, I walk the alley behind the apartments at 1214 & 1218 S. Farmer Avenue. It is a warm, starry night. In backyards on both sides of the alley in the darkness we can see tables & candles, hear conversations & laughter. I remark that this particular spot on the planet represents to me the center of the earth. I feel a deep joy to be there.

23 Oct 98: Walking with students on the east side of Mill Avenue near the Tempe Bridge. On the side of a building there is an engraved bronze plaque depicting the original territorial buildings of downtown Tempe. One of the students expresses incredulity that such buildings were deliberately demolished. I proceed to tell him the whole sorry tale.

31 Oct 98: We have rented an apartment at 7th Street & Forest Avenue. Strolling the streets, I am gladdened & gratified to be here again. And now, seeking a place in which to eat lunch, we enter Pete's Fish & Chips at 820 S. Mill Avenue. The grill is splattering with frying hamburgers. The customers are singing "The Unchained Melody." There is a pleasant, companionable atmosphere in this hallowed old greasy spoon. I remember that just across the alley within only 10 yards or so stands "the hovel," in which we once lived.

5 Nov 98: Walking west on the south side of Broadway Road. Looking north across the street, I can see Roosevelt Avenue & Clark Park. I sigh to recall all the many associations I have with this area, all the many memories I have. To the s.w. in the distance, I can see Bell Butte. In

search of a job, I'm bound for the Unemployment Office which is located in the distance on Industrial Park Avenue.

10 Dec 98: I stand outside the Language & Literature building on the ASU campus talking with the former chairman of the English Department. He promises to manoeuvre & manipulate procedures in such a way that I will be given an administrative position with the department. Ah, this will enable me to live in Tempe!

2 Jan 99: We walk the alley that runs from, 12th to 13th Street, between S. Farmer Avenue & Wilson Avenue. We're searching for an apartment to rent. And now, we consider one of those cinder block apartments that are located just east of the r.r. tracks on the north side of 13th Street. This would be acceptable. The campus & Tempe Center & the downtown would still be accessible (i.e. walkable) from here.

11 Jan 99: From somewhere south of the city, I'm being driven to Tempe. There are, however, mishaps & minor accidents that impede our progress.

13 Jan 99: Having returned to live in Tempe, I ride with a friend through the evening streets. 6th Street & Forest. Mill Avenue. Then west of Mill on 2nd Street. We enter a new tavern built on the site of an older bar. I ask the barman if when the present bar was built anything was found beneath the old wooden floor: an old coin, perhaps, an old newspaper? No, he informs me, nothing was found there.

7 Mar 99: So pleased to be here. Studying the façade of Tempe Hardware building at 520 S. Mill Avenue.

17 Mar 99: Having secured a good apartment on S. Farmer Avenue, I embark on a walk north along Farmer, cross University, turn right (east) on 4th Street & walk to the Casa Vieja. I enter Tempe Beach Park & see with sorrow that the stone WPA benches have been razed & removed. A sign informs me that the park is to be converted into a golf course. I

walk beneath the Tempe Bridge & will now proceed to climb Tempe Butte.

17 May 99: I pass (on my right) Campus Drugs at 660 S. College Avenue. I walk south on College, turn right on University, sit in an outdoor café at the All Saints Newman Center at 230 E. University Drive. Then, I walk north on Forest Avenue to 6th Street.

1 Jul 99: I'm walking south on the east side of Ash Avenue, between 6th Street & University Drive. I come upon a large new box-like building all shiny & inert. It has, of course, been constructed upon the former site of handsome old houses. "Annihilation by blandness."

16 Sep 99: On the east side of Mill Avenue, walking north, passing the Jack-in-the-Box, remembering with wistful affection their infamous tacos.

8 Oct 99: We have secured a rental at 1218 S. Farmer Avenue & are cleaning the sidewalk & area behind (to the s.) of our apartment, hosing it down. We plan to host a party this evening & in preparation we are positioning chairs, bowls, statues.

24 Oct 99: Living again at the 1214-1218 S. Farmer Avenue apartments. I have long wished to talk with the present occupant of the Judd house at 1208 S. Farmer Avenue. He is an elderly man. He moves slowly from chore to chore on his property: weeding, watering. Now he squats at the north end of his backyard, sorting vegetables from his garden: large red tomatoes, avocadoes, onions, cucumbers. I approach him from the alley & compliment him on his tomatoes. He offers me a few. I explain that I have always admired the house where he now lives & that when I lived next door in the late 1960s & early 70s, I used to greet the old couple – Orion & Anna Judd – who lived there then. The present occupant remarks to me that he has some notes on them. He is very friendly.

10 Nov 99: Returned to Tempe & living in the old apartments on S. Farmer Avenue. I walk to Tempe Center, recline on the grass there. I note with alarm the increasing number of offices occupying premises in Tempe Center & I fear that the whole center will ultimately be razed. Now, I walk west along the north side of 10th Street west of Mill Avenue. I am intent upon every detail of what is before me: the earth & grass, the alley, a wooden telephone pole, the asphalt street, the houses. I am immensely moved & grateful to be here. I can hardly comprehend that at long, long last I have returned to live in Tempe. I am thrilled to contemplate the explorations of streets & alleys & the railroad tracks that I will be now be able to undertake.

24 Nov 99: Having lived for a time on S. Farmer Avenue, I must now depart. I'm profoundly reluctant to leave. But now, I'm riding in a car, being driven away from Tempe. On the car radio, the Drifters are singing "Save the Last Dance for Me."

27 Nov 99: We have returned to Tempe, renting an apartment on the s.w. corner of 12th Street & S. Farmer Avenue. But now we have the opportunity to rent our former apartment at 1214 and a half S. Farmer, No. 1, in the two-story, gray building behind the house that fronts the street. I am deeply pleased at the prospect of doing so. Via the alley, we walk to the front door of the apartment, which I open with a key given to me by the landlord. Entering, I note that the same dark red carpeting still covers the floor.

30 Nov 99: Having returned to live on S. Farmer Avenue, I walk with companions east on the north side of 13th Street, then turn left (north) on Mill Avenue. As we walk through the downtown area, I comment on the new buildings there, expressing contempt for their flaccid homogeneity, their corny, faux frontier touches. We pass the Hayden Flour mill, a car dealership, & cross Tempe Bridge to the n. bank of the dry Salt River. I remark to my companions that what I like about Tempe is that it is a walkable city. Now, we turn around to return to the city. I plan to browse in Changing Hands bookshop on Mill Avenue.

21 Dec 99: Standing on the west side of Mill Avenue at 5th Street, talking to some people who inform me that there is a plan on the part of the mayor & city council to flood the area around the Hayden Flour mill. Furthermore, there is a proposal to change the color of Tempe Butte, dyeing it red in order to make it appear more picturesque. I object vehemently & argue against what I see as foolhardy, tasteless & wrong-headed notions.

25 Dec 99: We are sitting in the Valley Art Theatre. The film has not yet begun. I admire the multi-colored art deco lamps on the walls.

27 Jan 00: I feel keen disappointment & sorrow as I learn that we have to leave Tempe. I thought we had returned there to live. It is for me an uprooting in the strictest sense, as if the roots of my being were being pulled from the ground in which they are nourished.

28 Jan 00: I have spent the long day walking the streets of Tempe & now it is late afternoon. I'm walking east on the north side of University Drive at Myrtle Avenue. I note with sadness that to my left (north) construction is in progress on large bare building sites. Yet do I rejoice to be here. I exult, spreading my arms wide as if to embrace all that I see, while praying silently that I may return here to live.

9 Feb 00: Sitting again in the Valley Art Theatre. "On earth again of home." Fulfilled.

16 Mar 00: We are walking the alley that runs from 9th Street to 10th Street, between S. Maple Avenue & S. Ash Avenue. The backyards we view are so attractive, so interesting. I plan to walk s. on Ash from 10th to 13th Street, to see again the horse corral I once saw there.

27 Mar 00: Walking west on the north side of University Drive, near the intersection with Mill Avenue. This, I remember, is where a flower shop was once located. I bought flowers & a tall ceramic vase here once long

ago. Now I will walk to my apartment on S. Farmer Avenue near 13th Street.

3 Apr 00: We are living in an apartment on the east side of S. Farmer Avenue near 13th Street. The r.r. tracks run just behind the building in which we live. A man who runs a garage near 2nd Street west of Mill Avenue has offered me a job. I put on my field jacket preparing to accompany him to his shop.

5 Apr 00: Walking south on the west side of Mill Avenue, near 3rd Street. I plan to browse in Changing Hands Bookshop.

22 Apr 00: Living again in former apartment at 1218 S. Farmer Avenue. I visit our neighbors living in the Judd house next door. I tell them of the old couple (the Judds) who lived here in the late 60s & early 70s & of the two tall old date palm trees that grew in the front yard then (the stumps of which still remain.) I express my concern about the ultimate fate of the house & property, fearing that some developer will contrive to purchase the lot, demolish the house & build an apartment complex on the ground. And now, in fulfilment of one of my most cherished dreams, I am admitted to the interior of the house. How amazing & how wonderful to stand inside this house, beneath this roof, within these walls, looking out of these windows! Truly, this is a dream come true.

3 May 00: Visiting Tempe, walking along the west side of Mill Avenue just across the street from the Valley Art Theatre. Ah, the sight of the Valley Art arouses in me feelings of tenderness & affection. Above the marquee, I see the bas-relief figure of an angel. And now, in near despair I cling with my arms & legs to a lamppost, weeping & lamenting & crying out: "Oh, why can't I have a world, a life?"

20 May 00: I walk south on the east side of Mill Avenue onto the asphalt parking lot of Tempe Center. I look with favor & interest at the shops there. And now, onto the ASU campus, Orange Mall, the fountain, the Hayden Library.

11 Jun 00: I stand at the counter in the Moeur Building, seeking an information folder. Then, I wander north along Cady Mall to College Avenue & turn west on 6th Street.

29 Jun 00: Standing on Mill Avenue at about 5th Street, I feel outrage & indignation over the continuing destruction of historic buildings, the loss of authentic, romantic Tempe.

30 Jun 00: Walking north on the west side of S. Farmer Avenue near 13th Street. Approaching the intersection, I remember the tamarisk tree that once stood there. I cross 13th, continuing along the west side of Farmer, making a close, fond examination of each house I pass, trying to memorize every detail of what I am seeing. I note sadly that one house has been converted into a business office. This seems ominous.

10 Jul 00: Walking east on 10th Street, on the north side of the street, between Maple Avenue & Mill Avenue. Cross Mill Avenue & walk Tempe Center. Music is playing from within Tower Records at the s.e. corner of the strip mall. Jam's Restaurant is still operative. The grocery store (formerly El Rancho now Low Cost) is still up & running, as is also Appetito's Restaurant. Now, I break down, sobbing, overcome with grief & loss. All the years that have passed. "I can't take it," I cry.

26 Jul 00: I groan to see the devastation wrought by developers & urban renewal upon the Maple, Ash & Farmer quarter north of University Drive. This area once so fertile & resonant & mysterious is now sanitized, depthless & inert. As we cross University continuing south on Farmer Avenue, I become appreciative & responsive to the old trees & houses. We pass 1208 S. Farmer Avenue & I remark that if only I could afford to do so I would buy that little house & live there. That is my dream. To myself, I think: this is my proper place, this is for me the center of the earth. Now, we view the front apartment at 1218 S. Farmer Avenue & we are so taken with it that we determine to rent it. We will move our things from Denmark & live here. An exhilarating sense of new beginnings sweeps through me. I will again walk these streets!

13 Aug 00: In a strange, lovely red dusk I stand outside the Judd house at 1208 S. Farmer Avenue where there is an Indian festival in progress. There is music & dancing. I have taken an apartment next door at 1214. The red light of this dusk is so arresting that I exclaim aloud in praise.

24 Aug 00: Staying temporarily in an apartment at 1218 S. Farmer Avenue. I look around me at the walls, the floor & windows & silently cry: oh why can't I stay here?

25 Sep 00: Night in Tempe as we walk north along the east side of Forest Avenue at 7th Street. We stop to eat at a pleasant corner restaurant. I think that I now have the possibility to enter the Valley Art Theatre. Like anyone else in the world I could walk up to the ticket office, purchase a ticket & enter. And I would be there. I would actually & really & truly be there.

30 Sep 00: We are living temporarily in one of the apartments at 1214-1218 S. Farmer Avenue. I stroll down Farmer to 13th Street, turn right, then turn right again into the alley that runs from 13th to 12th between Wilson & Farmer. At long, long, long last I am again here in Tempe. I make a silent prayer that this time I can stay here. I can feel around me the aura or spirit or force field of the place. How strange that this alley, the sky above, the air, the earth, the stones here have not known my presence for so many years.

25 Oct 00: From east Phoenix, walk to Tempe. In the distance, I can see the Hayden Flour Mill & downtown buildings.

5 Nov 00: From Orange Mall on ASU campus, walk north along Cady Mall. To a companion I point out the Hayden Library, the Social Science building, the Language & Literature building. I intend to enter the L. & L. building to walk the corridors, see the classrooms.

11 Nov 00: It is a poignant moment. We have loaded our belongings in a car & are soon to drive away from our apartment at 1214 and a half South

Farmer Avenue, No. 1. I take a last look at my surroundings, attempting to imprint firmly & indelibly in my memory the things I now see.

13 Nov 00: Having returned to live in the apartments at 1214-1218 S. Farmer Avenue, I remark to my companion that for me the happiest thought is that henceforth every day I can walk Farmer Avenue.
18 Nov 00: We have rented the Judd house at 1208 S. Farmer Avenue! I mention to visitors that I have always wanted to live in this house, imagined & dreamed of doing so for many years.

5 Dec 00: I'm jogging on the ASU campus, south of the fountain on Cady Mall. I am stirred within by anticipation of jogging across University to College Avenue, past St. Mary's Church, past Campus Drugs & the book shops. Then, of a sudden, I am struck with the joyous revelation that I am in Tempe! I am really here! In grateful jubilation, I raise my arms to the heavens in a hosannah gesture. I am really here in Tempe & it is really here in every direction all around me, the houses, the streets, the alleys!

6 Dec 00: Walk with a companion from Tempe Center to the west side of Mill Avenue at 10th Street, turn right, walking north toward University Drive.

10 Dec 00: Cross Mill Avenue from east to west at 5th Street, proceed north to the south bank of the dry Salt River. I discover there the remnants of an original Hayden's Ferry homestead, a long-abandoned small holding with a low stone fence & wooden posts. An intriguing & mysterious find dating from the late 19th or early 20th century. Imbued with history, it has endured the weathers & occasional floods all these many years.

18 Dec 00: East of Tempe at fall of dark. I'll soon be going downtown. I feel anticipatory excitement.

23 Jan 01: Renting apartment no. 3 at 1218 S. Farmer Avenue. I take a walk around the block: Farmer to 13th then right (west) to Wilson Avenue, right (north) on Wilson, right (east) on 12th Street to Farmer. I so admire the houses along Wilson. Seeing all this gives me great pleasure. And soon I will be walking the alleys!

23 Feb 01: It is the first hour of the first day of our return to Tempe, to an apartment at 1218 S. Farmer Avenue. In happiness & satisfaction, I walk Farmer to 13th, turn right (west) walk a few yards then pause to look down & study the spot where the cement sidewalk meets the stony alley. It is a threshold of a kind, I conclude. An appropriate symbol of this day & hour when I am crossing a threshold, beginning a new phase of my life. As a personal ritual, a gesture to be remembered, I step from the sidewalk into the alley.

2 Apr 01: I'm being driven west on 10th Street between Mill Avenue & S. Farmer Avenue. As the car speeds along (the driver heedless of our surroundings) I relish – as best I can – the individual, charming, desirable houses I can see.

1 Jun 01: Standing near the alley behind 1218 S. Farmer Avenue. I gaze with interest into a ditch that has been dug there by the city in order to lay or replace some pipe. I am eager to examine the ditch more closely, search carefully for an artefact of Tempe's past.

28 Jul 01: At the n.w. corner of 10th Street & Mill Avenue. I stand attempting to memorize every detail of the objects before my eyes: buildings on campus, Tempe Center, grass & palm trees, the cement curb, the black asphalt street. Then, turning around, I see the alley that runs from University Drive to 10th Street, between Maple Avenue & Mill. I will enjoy the adventure of walking there later. Now walking west on 10th Street, I come to the n.e. corner of Maple & from a tree growing near the sidewalk there I take a few leaves, rolling them between my fingers. I want to feel their texture, inhale their fragrance. I exclaim aloud: "I am here! I am here!"

6 Sep 01: I am looking at a photograph of Tempe but then I am there. I see Tempe Butte, Tempe Bridge, the Casa Loma.

15 Sep 01: I am sitting in the dark in the Valley Art Theatre. The film has not yet begun. I look with pleasure on the walls, the seats, the screen.
21 Nov 01: We have just concluded an agreement with a landlord for an apartment on the west side of Ash Avenue near 10th Street. I tell the landlord that Tempe is the best place I have ever lived.

3 Dec 01: Returned to live in Tempe at 1218 S. Farmer Avenue, no. 3. With tears in my eyes, I contemplate all the many years I yearned to return here. My dearest wish, my deepest dream, for so long has been to walk Farmer Avenue.

29 Dec 01: Having just now moved into our old apartment at 1218 S. Farmer Avenue, I now want to undertake a delicious, deliberate walk through my heart's hometown. I begin in the alley, taking in the specific particulars of the backyards & houses, the trees & stones. I am conscious of having long desired to do just this. Next, I want to walk Ash between 13th & 10th Streets. Ah! I'm mesmerized, inebriated.

17 Jan 02: We have rented a little house on Maple Avenue just north of 10th Street.

1 Feb 02: Returned to our former apartment on S. Farmer Avenue, I commence a walk north along Farmer. I study the houses across the street, appreciating their individual accent, their modesty, their simple charm. I note, however, the intrusion of one new building there, a bland & unattractive structure. And now with sorrow I see that the Judd house at 1208 S. Farmer Avenue has been demolished! Only piles of brown dirt remain on the lot. What a great pity this is!

22 Feb 02: A very brief visit to Tempe. Standing on the east side of Mill Avenue at 7th Street, I look north along Mill observing with sad disapproval the many bland new buildings that have been constructed

on both sides of the street. I have the afternoon hours planned: a walk west on 10th to S. Farmer Avenue, then back & forth along Maple & Ash Avenues, to the campus, to St. Mary's Church.

24 Mar 02: West of Mill Avenue at 6th Street. Featureless sameness yet poetic possibilities persist.

19 Apr 02: Returned, rented former flat at 1218. I embark upon my first walk in Tempe. Farmer north to 12th Street, walk west past Wilson, Roosevelt. Attentive, appreciative. Colored wash hanging on a clothes line. The sense of deep affinity. And now I turn around to walk back to our apartment.

21 Apr 02: Riding a passenger train to Tempe. I look out of the window at the familiar Arizona landscape: cacti, weeds, brown earth, purple mountains. Anticipatory excitement.

16 Jun 02: Walking on the east side Mill Avenue at the north end of the city, near the Hayden Flour Mill & Tempe Bridge. Intrigued by Pueblo-style buildings I come upon there. If they are not authentic, they are at least handsome & convincing imitations.

22 Jul 02: Living again in no. 3 at 1218 S. Farmer Avenue. I set off to walk to the Hayden Library. En route, I note some changes have taken place in the quarter, certain alterations have been made to some houses & lawns. The changes are within the realm of acceptability.

12 Aug 02: I'm walking homeward to an apartment we have rented near the dry Salt riverbed, walking east on the north side of 13th just past Wilson Avenue. I gaze wistfully into the alley that runs from 13th to 12th, between Wilson & Farmer. I am swept with nostalgia remembering the occasion when we returned here in September of 1971 & went for a walk in the alley & saw there a tall sunflower. And now, I am amazed & pleased suddenly to meet some of our old neighbors.

14 Sep 02: Gazing at the night sky in Tempe. In the west, I see Arcturus.

4 Jan 03: Returned to Tempe & living at 1214 and a half S. Farmer
Avenue No. 1. I stand on Farmer facing west, gazing at the Judd House.
A middle-aged woman, the new owner, potters about the yard, pulling a
few weeds. I speak to her, praising her house, expressing my great relief
that the house was purchased rather than razed. I tell her how lovely her
house looks in the soft light of a winter dawn or in the early hours of a
summer morning. Even now, looking at it, I feel a mixture of wonder &
pleasure.

9 Feb 03: With two companions, I stroll the concrete sidewalk of Tempe
Center. We pass Ray's ASU Barbershop & through the glass window I
can see within the barber chairs & busy barbers. Now, we pass the
supermarket (formerly El Rancho currently Low Cost) & within I can see
the cashiers & customers. I experience a sudden rush of perceptual
intensity & I concentrate on every detail. I am so very pleased to be here
& relieved that Tempe Center is still intact.

15 Feb 03: I walk from S. Farmer Avenue to the ASU campus. I find the
sunlight & the warm air most agreeable. And (despite the sight of a new
tall lacklustre rectangular building in the downtown area) I find being
here very pleasant, indeed.

9 Apr 03: We have just moved into an apartment west of Mill Avenue at
3rd Street & Roosevelt. In the fading light of early evening, I take a walk,
heading east then north. I exult to see the red light of evening touching
distant mountains. I walk a path near the Casa Vieja then decide to
return to our apartment. I love this walk & all that I see & I take pleasure
in the knowledge that I can see all of this again & again, day after day.

17 Apr 03: Visiting Tempe, walking west on 13th Street, on the north side
of the street, just west of S. Farmer Avenue. I turn right (north) into the
alley. Closely & carefully, I study the stones, the gravel, the backs of the
houses & their backyards. I weep to be here & to see it all again. I wish &

wish & wish I could live here. Why may I not? Why can't I? I have rented for a few days the Judd house at 1208 S. Farmer Avenue & I'm very eager to enter & experience this house that has attracted me for so long. I turn my key in the door & step across the threshold. The linoleum on the floor is antique, a swirling marbled pattern of red & brown. Placed here & there in the wooden walls are colored tiles. Empty of furniture the little house is a time capsule of the early 20th century. I wonder who will buy it & what will become of it? I move from room to room devoting unhurried & meticulous attention to each detail of the walls & floors. Oh, how I would love to live here! For so many years I have desired nothing more desperately than to live in this house. I look through an east-facing window. Now I know what the interior of this house looks like & what it is like to see Tempe through these windows. I am deeply moved & highly excited & vividly alive.

26 Apr 03: Returned to Tempe to live there. Walking with a companion on the east side of Ash Avenue just before it intersects with 10th Street.

1 May 03: It is early morning & I'm jogging south on the west side of Mill Avenue between 9th & 10th Streets. As I jog across 10th, I look to my right & see that it has snowed! The ground & trees are white with snow. It is a lovely scene & I feel wonder & delight.

28 May 03: I walk west with companions on the south side of University Drive, proceeding past Maple & Ash Avenues & the old house where once there was a used bookshop. I want to guide my companions south along S. Farmer Avenue to show them the interesting houses there. Afterward, we can walk Ash & Maple between 13th & 10th Streets. Mysterious, magnetic Tempe.

28 July 03: Visiting Tempe, walking past the Judd House at 1208 S. Farmer Avenue, observing it with wistful attention. Then, I notice that the front door is open so that I can see the interior. Oh, the fascination & allure!

21 Aug 03: A visit to Tempe. From a tower in the Maple/Ash quarter I have a splendid view of the surrounding streets, the houses & backyards & sheds. I am swept with elation & attraction & simultaneously with sorrow for I fear that all this will be destroyed. I wish I had lived here. I must live here.

22 Oct 03: Guiding my companions on a walk of Tempe, we are just turning right off the west side of Mill Avenue at 10th Street. I feel keen excitement at the prospect of seeing again this neighborhood so dear to me in memory. As we turn onto 10th Street, however, the whole of the street all the way west to S. Farmer Avenue is blocked by a gigantic yellow-brown ceramic funnel that has been placed in the street by the city council as an artistic "improvement." I feel frustration & helpless sorrow. To my companions I remark: of all the streets in all the towns & cities of the world, I loved 10th Street the best.

29 Nov 03: I have just turned right from S. Farmer Avenue onto 13th Street. And now I want to recreate in actual physical space the imaginary runs I made around our small apartment in Copenhagen, envisioning as I jogged every detail that I would see if I were in Tempe. I jog past the alley, the curb, Wilson Avenue, past each remembered house, sighing in my soul to see it all. As I continue west along 13th Street I remember, too, a long ago morning in late May when I walked this way, alive with hope & happiness.

4 Jan 04: Together with companions, I'm being driven in a car west on University Drive, west of Mill Avenue. We pass Maple & Ash Avenues, then S. Farmer Avenue. To my companions, I point out the unique charms of the houses we pass (all too quickly.) Some are humble but handsome and honest, some stately, all are picturesque. But it is clear to me from the lack of replies from the others in the car that I am alone in responding to the romance of these old houses. Such is the deadening effect of "the automobilized mind," that never experiences life at 3 miles per hour.

22 Jan 04: Walking together with an old man north on the west side of Mill Avenue at 5th Street. Now we come to the gutted shell of the building where illustrious, legendary Parry's Bar stood. The ceiling is gone & everything has been stripped from the interior. The rest of the building will soon be demolished. On the floor along the south wall you can still make out an outline of where the bar was placed. In sadness, I enter the ruin. I want to stand one last time in this hallowed space.

12 Mar 04: Walking Tempe Center with companions. I am relieved & pleased to see that the Center is intact. Indeed, there are now fewer offices & more shops. I discourse to my companions about the history & the current fate of strip malls in the United States. Ah, now, I enter the laundromat at the north end of the Center. This is a moment of nostalgic pleasure for me, as I used to do our laundry here regularly when we lived in Tempe. The sound of the tumblers, the clean smell, the table where I used to fold our clothes, the wooden bench where I used to sit.

7 May 04: Accompanied by two companions, I walk the parking lot & sidewalk of Tempe Center, starting at the northern end of the shops. I note a sidewalk performance of magical arts, a store-front mosque, offices where once there were shops. The old "T.G.&Y." variety store is gone, replaced by something utterly banal. I remember the morning when I woke in our new flat in Tempe ("the hovel") & crossed Mill Avenue & bought cheap white china tea mugs here. We continue our walk in the direction of the supermarket (originally El Rancho, later Stapler's, then Low Cost.) If it is gone then living in or near downtown Tempe would be complicated. But I am consoled to see that it is still there. I remember when I first shopped here. An employee assures me that the store will remain at Tempe Center. Now, we walk to the east side of Mill Avenue, witnessing another display of the magical arts. Looking back (east) across Mill Avenue at Tempe Center, I tell my companions of my deep, powerful & long-standing yearning to return to Tempe. Unable to restrain myself, I sob & weep.

13 Jun 04: Returned to live in Tempe: an apartment on the s.w. corner of 12th Street & S. Farmer Avenue, then an apartment on Wilson Avenue. Now, I stand contemplating with pleasure & covetous craving the Judd house at 1208 S. Farmer Avenue. Standing near me on the sidewalk is a middle-aged woman with whom I initiate a conversation, telling her how very much I like the house. She informs me that she & her husband & children live there, they're renting it. She employs a slightly disparaging adjective in describing the house. Now, her husband & children emerge from the house. They are 8 in number. (It must be rather crowded for them in there.) I talk to the husband about my avid admiration for the house, my acquaintance long ago with the Judds, & how I have so often dreamed of the house during my many years of living abroad.

4 Aug 04: On a visit to Tempe, I try to replicate walks I took long ago, to see what I saw then, be where I was then. I stroll the west side of S. Farmer Avenue, north of 10th Street to University Drive. There, I cross to the east side of Farmer & walk south. Every detail of what I see is to me so ineffably fascinating: porches, windows, doors, roofs, fences. My eyes must long ago have brushed the very objects I now see.

13 Sep 04: Returned to Tempe for a brief stay, I have rented an apartment on the south side of 13th Street between Ash Avenue & Farmer, near the r.r. tracks. I walk the alley that runs from 13th to 12th Streets, between Wilson Avenue & S. Farmer Avenue. I am mesmerized with admiration. I examine carefully the things before me. I am drawn powerfully to this place. The thought seizes me: "Oh, why did I ever leave?"

15 Oct 04: I have received a grant to study the Judd House at 1208 S. Farmer Avenue. The amount of the grant will enable me to remain in Tempe for weeks, perhaps months. It is early morning as I approach the Judd House. The residents within are not yet awake. I feel excitement, attraction, anticipation. I pitch a tent on the bare earth to the north of the house. This will be the base for my research. Now, I see that the

residents of the house have awoken & risen from their beds. I can see them walking past the curtained windows. I am eager to begin.

29 Oct 04: Returned to Tempe & returned to our former apartment at 1218 S. Farmer Avenue. I'm driven in a car north on S. Farmer Avenue. I look eagerly out of the car window as we pass the houses I so admire & I attempt to point out to the driver & passengers the individual beauty of each house, but the car is moving so quickly that the others scarcely have time to take a glance at the houses. I think with pleasure of the downtown. But now I catch a bus back to S. Farmer Avenue, sitting up front with the driver with whom I discuss the changes in the city. I am dismayed to see that the charming wooden houses on the east side of Farmer near 13th have been torn down & replaced with concrete apartment complexes. Nevertheless, much that I love remains. I can scarcely believe that I am really here. I feel such gratitude & such deep joy. I weep & weep with joy.

8 Nov 04: A short visit to Tempe, seeing again the streets so dear to me. I stare with fascination, hoping to commit to memory every detail of what I see. I remark to my companion that these vivid moments are of value to me, like Wordsworth's awareness in "Tintern Abbey" that "in this moment there is life & food for future years." But when I think of the long years ahead, I feel a near despair.

24 Nov 04: On a visit to Tempe. I am standing at the n.w. corner of S. Myrtle Avenue & 10th Street. I am looking to find the cement contractor's stamp in the sidewalk that I used to see here long ago. (John W. Lattimore/Contractor/1955)

10 Dec 04: Using a long measuring tape to determine & record distances on the lot on which the Judd House sits. Discussing with collaborators on this project the stumps of the two palm trees that once grew here.

3 Jan 05: Smiling, energetic Sonny Rollins is peddling his bicycle westward along 13th Street just east of S. Farmer Avenue! I rejoice to see

him. This encounter will make the spot here not only memorable but forever sacred to me.

31 Jan 05: As we cross University Drive at Mill Avenue, heading north on the east side of Mill, I remember again the occasion on which I bought at a florist shop here long-stemmed roses & at a nearby ceramic shop a tall vase in which to put them. I want to see if the two shops still exist.

6 Feb 06: A salesman has given me a lift into Tempe. We park at the Travel Lodge Motel at 9th Street & Mill Avenue. I am extolling to him the charms of Tempe but I perceive that the salesman is utterly indifferent to my claims. Moreover, he clearly finds the Travel Lodge Motel to be beneath his usual standard of accommodation.

27 Feb 05: Long, leisurely & most pleasant reacquaintance with the streets & houses from University Drive to 13th Street, between Mill Avenue & S. Farmer Avenue. I pass the intriguing alleys, thinking that I will explore them soon.

8 Mar 05: Mr. & Mrs. Judd (Orion & Anna) have dug a cinema in the front yard of their house at 1208 S. Farmer Avenue. The cinema consists of a rectangular hole in the earth about 20 feet long by 12 feet wide. The Judds screen oldtime movies here, quite innocent slapstick comedies from the silent era. I descend into the hole, thrilled to be *beneath* Tempe. Later, I speak with Mrs. Judd telling her that I recall when there were two tall palm trees in their front yard. I take great pleasure in being here, doing this, seeing this.

9 Mar 05: On a visit to Tempe, I walk from Mill Avenue to College Avenue, from Tempe Butte to University Drive. I note with gratification that several very interesting old houses still remain on the streets of this quarter. "Redevelopment" has not yet been as extensive as I have feared. To a companion, I remark that I love Tempe, though that must be difficult for others to comprehend. I love it. It exercises upon me a power of attraction that I can't communicate to others. To others a walk

such as this is of little interest or consequence, but I am filled with happiness to be here.

15 Mar 05: We ask to be let off on the east side of Mill Avenue at 10th Street. I am very much looking forward to walking the ASU campus, seeing St. Mary's Church & College Avenue, then strolling west on 6th Street to Mill Avenue.

21 Apr 05: I'm saddened to see alterations that have been made to the backyard of the apartments at 1214-1218 S. Farmer Avenue. A large hole has been dug there, the wall enclosing the backyard has been torn down.

18 Jun 05: Very charming, very bohemian apartment occupied by an old acquaintance & his wife on the south side of 10th Street near Mill Avenue. I believe that this house is where a modest Beauty Parlor was located in the late 1960s. I view the kitchen, the bedroom, a studio for painting. I feel a sharp pang of envy. This place is perfect & it is so very near to my much cherished Hayden Library.

21 Jun 05: Waiting for a moving van to take our belongings as we depart Tempe. I stand on the n.w. corner of 10th Street & Myrtle Avenue. I wander off to a patch of weedy ground on the west side of Myrtle. This unnoticed, insignificant plot of ground will henceforward be a kind of fixed point for me, it will be hallowed forever in my memory, a datum of desire.

15 Jul 05: From every direction around me, the mysterious, magnetic current of old Tempe, evoking in me a sympathetic communion.

29 Jul 05: In desperate suspense, I run to the 1200 block of S. Farmer Avenue. I must know if the destructive incursions of developers have reached this far. To my deep relief, all is still intact. Indeed, a protective metal structure (like that preserving the Casa Grande ruins) has been built above the Judd House. I wish so fervently that I could remain here

& live here, but I know I cannot. It is impossible. I take hold of a cluster of leaves from a nearby tree, clutching them in my hand. I shed tears of loss & longing.

5 Sep 05: At nightfall, together with a companion, I turn west from Mill Avenue onto the north side of 10th Street. With attention & deep appreciation, I scrutinize the houses & trees. I feel excitement & a kind of awe but my companion talks on & on, oblivious to our surroundings. Dark tree leaves beneath a darkening sky. Silently, I say to myself: "Oh, this is good!"

28 Oct 05: With an aim to renting a room, we are visiting an old couple who live in a house in the Maple/Ash neighbourhood. They open the door of the room so that we can see it before making our decision. How interesting & stimulating for me to see this particular enclosed space. It has existed through the years & now I am here & seeing it.

29 Oct 05: I have been telling my companion of my enduring attraction to Tempe, of my many years of yearning, of my numerous night-dreams of the place. To enact a recurrent dream I have had, I stand in the middle of the street where 9th Street intersects Maple Avenue & raise my arms above my head in exaltation. How strange it is to perform in real life an act I have performed in dreams. And now dusk is falling in the streets of Tempe & I am really here.

3 Nov 05: I have somehow been transported back in time to the year 1905. I stand on bare brown desert earth to the n.w. of distant Mill Street with its half-dozen scattered two-story buildings. I follow a dirt road which runs east toward Tempe Butte & Mill Street. And now, I'm riding along Mill Street, reclining in the back of wagon. I can only see the upper third of the buildings as we pass rapidly southward along the street, but I can recognize certain of them from the Tempe that I knew in the 1960s & early 1970s. I study them intently, taking mental notes on styles, features, characteristics, building materials.

26 Nov 05: I am walking west on the south side of 10th Street, south of Ash Avenue. And now I cross the r.r. tracks & turn left (south) on the east side of S. Farmer Avenue. My spirit quickens to see the many houses I love, which yet remain as I have so often remembered them. At length, I arrive at 12th Street & near the place that is always at the center of my heart. I cross Farmer to view the old Judd House & the apartments at 1214-1218 S. Farmer Avenue but midway across the street, I kneel & kiss the asphalt. I'm weeping both with joy & loss. This is, for me, the center of the earth.

26 Dec 05: Walking east on a dirt path toward Tempe Butte. Behind me the sun is setting & I note that my shadow is cast onto the side of the butte. I move my hand & wave my arm, watching my huge dark shadow on the butte do likewise. I continue walking east toward the butte, the sun behind me.

29 Dec 05: I stand on the west side of Mill Avenue at 9th Street. The Travel Lodge motel has been demolished, only the empty swimming pool remains. Looking across the street, I see that Tempe Center, too, has been razed & replaced by new buildings proclaiming "the Gateway to ASU."

It is early morning as I stand on the sidewalk examining the Judd House at 1208 S. Farmer Avenue. I relish every detail of the roof & windows, the door & façade. Walking along the southern perimeter of the lot on which the house stands, I note a boundary marker set in the earth. It is a short, rounded concrete pillar, decorated with a stylized wreath of leaves. The marker dates from the construction of the house in 1915 & has stood here steadfastly all these many years through the fierce summer heat & the starry winter nights.

2 Jan 06: Walking north on Forest Avenue, north of University Drive.

15 Jan 06: I am standing on the west side of Mill Avenue at 9th Street, looking east across Mill Avenue to Tempe Center. The entire Center is

being remodelled. There is scaffolding & sheets of plastic in front of the shops, which now are closed. I am somewhat relieved to see that the original form of Tempe Center will be maintained though the shops that replace those that were there formerly will be upscale & exclusive. No more bookstore, record store, liquor store, dime store, drug store, restaurant, laudromat.

10 Feb 06: On a visit to Tempe, walking 6th Street, Myrtle Avenue, Forest Avenue. I feel the familiar fascination & attraction & sob with sadness & nostalgia. I enter a bookshop on the south side of 5th Street (east of Mill Avenue) & there find & purchase a copy of *The Dream Peddler* (1914) by Vita Sackville-West. I've long wished to own a copy. And now I walk to Tempe Bridge & out onto the bridge to the first cupola.

22 Feb 06: The Judd House has been lifted from its foundations & brought forward (east) toward S. Farmer Avenue. The house has been given a fresh coat of white paint. I fear that the house is to be removed from the site permanently & placed elsewhere, but perhaps it will be replaced on the foundation. I can see the now exposed stone & cement foundation & am very eager to have a look at it. The foundation has not seen the sunlight in many years, yet it has stood there (in secret, as it were) through the seasons & the weathers, through wars & eras. I do fear that this may be the end of this unique & charming house at 1208 S. Farmer Avenue & that some eager, venal developers will replace it with an apartment complex, something glossy & bland.

15 Mar 06: I must first take a long written examination, after which I can explore Tempe. I have only just arrived & my heart sinks to learn of this delay. But I feel a pleasant inward stirring at the prospect of walking the old neighborhoods.

20 Mar 06: Turn north from Broadway Road onto Mill Avenue, pass Tempe High School, left (west) on 13th & a right turn (north) on South

Farmer Avenue. To a companion, I remark: "I always liked to walk this street." And now we see an interesting used book shop.

24 Mar 06: Visiting Tempe, walking 6th Street east of Mill Avenue. I enter a book shop, chat with the owner about the callous destruction of old Tempe. I find an interesting paperbound book from 1904 with manila pages & covers, an account of adventures in India. It is stimulating & satisfying to browse here.

8 Apr 06: I ride a horse along an old dirt path into Tempe.

10 Apr 06: Together with companions, driven in a car south across Tempe Bridge onto Mill Avenue. It's a warm night. I remark that Tempe has been ruined but not entirely: the Casa Loma, Lairds, the André building, the Hardware building, the Valley Art Theatre still stand.

17 Apr 06: Walking south along the west side of Mill Avenue, a leisurely & pleasant browse of the shops.

19 Apr 06: We are living again at 1218 S. Farmer Avenue, though not in our former apartment there (but next door.) Rise early & buy delicious pastries at nearby bakery.

13 May 06: I stand in an empty apartment at 1218 S. Farmer Avenue. Then, I walk the old streets (10th, Ash, Maple) dismayed to see the inroads made in this neighborhood by callous & opportunistic developers. Slick, sterile new apartment complexes have been constructed among the older houses.

10 Jun 06: I stand on 6th Street, east of Mill Avenue & all around me, all of the structures have been razed. The final erasure of this quarter by commercial forces has been accomplished. I look around in grief & gloom but this brief interval between destruction & construction provides me with a unique glimpse of how this space below the butte must have looked in earliest Tempe: flat, vacant, dirt brown. And now I

walk to Mill Avenue & see that the exterior of the prized & precious Valley Art Theatre is being remodelled! This is abominable, intolerable!

15 Jun 06: We walk north on S. Farmer Avenue to a house on the n.w. corner of Farmer & University Drive. It is a small, very attractive bungalow. We view the rooms each of which is furnished simply & honestly. The colors within are cheerful but subtle. To the owner, we express our admiration for the house & its interior décor.

16 Jul 06: Alert & vividly alive, I stand on the n.w. corner of the intersection of S. Farmer Avenue & 13th Street. I can choose to walk east on 13th, turning north on Ash or Maple, or I can choose to walk north on Farmer. Such delightful options.

13 Aug 06: I am all packed to leave Tempe. To a companion I explain my sorrow & regret at leaving. But I am compelled to do so.

20 Aug 06: Somehow I have returned to a time in the 1960s. It's night in Tempe & I walk 5th & 6th Streets east of Mill Avenue. No-one is about. I am very excited, very interested by everything I see: the houses, the trees, the shops.

30 Aug 06: Frank Sinatra in Tempe! With a small entourage he's walking east on the south side of 5th Street, passing the American Legion Hall, behind which his car is parked. And now I am walking on the west side of Mill Avenue just across from the Valley Art Theatre with its colored neon sign glowing in the night. How handsome it is & how wonderful that it exists!

10 Oct 06: Walking the concrete sidewalk of Tempe Center, passing the space Tops Liquors once occupied. As I proceed north along the shops, in amazement I repeat silently to myself: it is all so familiar! So familiar! And then to myself I say: this is where I want to be. I want to stay here.

15 Oct 06: I climb to the top of Tempe Butte & gaze down onto Tempe upon what seems to me an almost Edenic beauty.

19 Oct 06: Up & down the alleys & streets of old Tempe I walk. Maple, Ash, Farmer. I am enraptured by the houses, fences, backyards, trees & telephone poles which seem to me magical, glorious, otherworldly & rich with mystery.

29 Oct 06: Together with a companion, I enter Tempe on a bus, riding south along Mill Avenue. I look out the window at the interesting shops as we pass. It is a sunny winter afternoon. The bus stops a bit south of 10th Street & when I look west along 10th the view is, I think to myself, as vivid & visionary as in my dreams. I anticipate wonderful hours of walking the neighborhoods so dear to me. Studying with approval an old house on Mill Avenue just south of 10th, I remark to my companion: "you have no idea how much I love this place. I *love* it."

12 Nov 06: My eyes full of tears, I gaze across Mill Avenue at the Travel Lodge Motel, the tall palm trees & the old houses with their porches.

15 Nov 06: A nostalgic pilgrimage to our old flat at 1218 S. Farmer Avenue, no. 3. The door is open & through the screen door I can see figures moving within the apartment. I knock on the door & identify myself by name & as a former tenant who now lives in Denmark. I show my passport & am allowed to enter. I have not stood in this space since August of 1972. I note that some interior remodelling has taken place. But here I am! This is the place, the space. "I've dreamed of this so often," I tell the occupant & her guest. And it is dreamlike being here. I gaze about myself in wonder. There is the bathroom, the closet, the walls. I can see now that the occupant is becoming bored with my enthusiasm & reminiscence so I take my leave. Almost immediately, I lose my way & wander the nearby streets, lost, looking to return to Farmer Avenue. Seeing a young woman ion the sidewalk, I inquire of her my way. She tells me of all the strata & soil types beneath this area of Tempe, the deep, unseen Precambrian depths. She knows well the

stratification of this area. She informs me that beneath S. Farmer Avenue & 13th Street there is an underground river & a large body of subsurface water. I wonder to myself if this might in some strange fashion account for my attraction to this area.

16 Nov 06: I disembark from a bus near 10th Street on the west side of Mill Avenue. In a state of high excitement I set off upon my nostalgic journey intending to walk west on 10th to Farmer & then south on Farmer. I note a field of wild flowers & a view of distant mountains but then realize with a start of sorrow that the field before me represents blocks of old houses that have been torn down. New construction will soon be underway here. Indeed, I see that construction equipment is already in place. On Farmer, too, all is destroyed. My beloved Tempe has been razed, erased.

17 Nov 06: Between Farmer & Wilson, south of 13th Street.

6 Jan 07: Strolling the alley that runs from 13th to 12th between Wilson & Farmer Avenues. Shelves of objects in an open-air warehouse behind 1222 S. Farmer Avenue. We have an opportunity to rent an apartment at 1218. I am filled with glad anticipation of our future life here.

13 Jan 07: Recurrence of (recurrent) dream of 6 Jan 07.

21 Jan 07: I approach the current occupant of apartment no. 4 at 1218 S. Farmer Avenue for permission to enter, explaining that friends lived here long ago. Within the apartment much has been altered but it is still recognizable & I feel a pleasant link to the past. I exit, turn south, walk the alley to 13th Street.

23 Jan 07: Standing on the sidewalk, gazing with yearning at 1214 & 1218 S. Farmer Avenue. Walk a few steps to the north & contemplate with infatuation the Judd House at 1208. I wish I could view the interior of the house. I determine to approach the owner in a little while. Meanwhile, I continue north on the east side of Farmer, regarding with

scrupulous, studious attention the houses on both sides of the street. In my spirit I feel such a sharp pang. I would stay here, if only I could. Knowing that it is impossible, I weep in the street.

1 Feb 07: I enter the Language & Literature building on the ASU campus. I will be taking a course from Professor O'Malley.

16 Feb 07: Fortune has smiled upon me & I have rented an apartment at 1214 and a half S. Farmer Avenue. The apartment is currently being renovated. There will be a wait before moving in.

17 Feb 07: Walking along the west side of Mill Avenue at 7th Street. I am eager to walk west on 10th Street.

4 Mar 07: Three strangers have given us a ride in their car to Tempe. At our request, they let us off at the north end of Tempe Center, near the laundromat. We walk the familiar cement sidewalk of the center, walking south toward the supermarket.

19 Mar 07: Joy, contentment, fulfilment, excitement. We are moving back into an apartment at 1214-1218 S. Farmer Avenue. Absorbed, entranced, I stand on the sidewalk looking west at the trees & facades.

27 Mar 07: On a visit to Tempe, walking south on the east side of Mill Avenue with the goal of seeing again the dear streets of the Maple/Ash/Farmer quarter. I feel the appeal, the pull of the place.

7 Apr 07: It is night in Tempe. I have just arrived & from the north side of University Drive a bit west of Mill Avenue, I hail a taxi cab. I want to see the old apartments on S. Farmer Avenue. As the driver turns south onto Farmer, I tell him of the powerful attraction I have felt for years to this place, my many night dreams of being here. And now alone, I approach our former residence at 1218 S. Farmer Avenue. The backyard wall, the water heaters, the cement sidewalk, the grass. I reflect that I could sleep here on the grass unseen in the darkness. I could pass a

warm night beneath the stars. And tomorrow I could talk to the current residents of the apartments & investigate every detail, every feature & aspect of the place: the earth, the plants, the bushes & cacti, the doors & windows.

25 Apr 07: With companions, I enter & seat myself in the Valley Art Theatre (near the wall at the north of the theatre.) There is the screen, the floor, the ceiling, the walls, there are the colored art deco lamps I love. As we are leaving the theatre, I note that one patron has written the date on the floor using a marker pen. I wonder how long it will remain.

22 May 07: I walk east with companions on the south side of 5th Street (e. of Mill Avenue.) As we pass the former site of the American Legion Hall, I speak of the musical events that took place there in years past. As we walk on, I point to the new buildings that have replaced old houses & shops. I see that the First Congregational Church on the s.e. corner of 6th Street & Myrtle & St. Mary's Church on University Drive remain. Forlorn fragments of the past.

27 Jun 07: The Judd House at 1208 S. Farmer Avenue is to be sold. I wonder if we could possibly borrow from a bank the money necessary to buy it. I stand in the alley studying the rear of the house & the wooden shed, imagining how amazing it would be to live in this house that has haunted my dreams for so long.

5 Jul 07: 6th Street & Myrtle Avenue. There has been a literary festival & I examine a poster listing the authors who took part in it.

21 Aug 07: We are well-located in an apartment on 9th Street near Maple Avenue, in the very heart of what remains of old Tempe. I am well pleased.

30 Aug 07: I stand in the dry river bed west of Tempe Bridge watching a procession of gravel trucks pass over the bridge & into Tempe. And now

I turn my gaze south to Mill Avenue. I anticipate with pleasure a long, slow walk down Mill Avenue & its adjacent side streets.

2 Nov 07: A pleasant sojourn in Tempe. I am restored.

9 Dec 07: The owners of the house (somewhere in Maple/Ash district) in which I am staying mention "the Rundles" who live just across the street. I am immediately intrigued, wondering whether they were not the owners of Rundle's Market – a place for me of such hallowed memory. If that is the case, then perhaps they may have some photographs of the store.

21 Dec 07: It is very dark, so I use my flashlight to light the way for a companion & myself onto the grounds of the Judd House which I have rented. I walk the yard, then recline on a couch in front of the house, enjoying the fine warm night.

29 Dec 07: I wish I had a camera but I'm doing my utmost to commit to memory every charming detail of what I'm seeing as I walk up & down, back & forth along Maple Avenue & Ash Avenue, between 10th Street & University Drive: the fences, the porches, the bushes, the trees, the WPA sidewalk. I note that encroachments of soulless "condos" have been made nearby & I fear that ultimately the whole quarter may be doomed.

15 Jan 08: I will rendezvous with a friend on the east side of St. Mary's Church, the side along College Avenue. We can then stroll the ASU campus & points west. The prospect excites & delights me.

20 Jan 08: I cross S. Farmer Avenue, walking from east to west, & enter our newly rented apartment in the house that fronts the street at 1218 S. Farmer Avenue. Boxes of our possessions are stacked in the rooms. We unpack our stereo so that we can hear music while we remove the contents of the other boxes. Later, there will be time to walk the streets. I feel that I have returned to my proper ground.

26 Jan 08: Watching a 1940s *Lassie* film. Lassie is walking along the cement railing of a long white bridge. It's Tempe Bridge! I can see the cupolas. And in the background of the shot can be seen Tempe Butte & the Hayden Flour Mill! Now, the camera moves along 1940s Mill Avenue, the Casa Loma, the old territorial buildings with their stepped gables. Now I know why that vintage colored postcard I own depicting 1940s Mill Avenue shows the marquee of the College Theatre advertising *Lassie Come Home.*

16 Mar 08: I am enormously pleased to be present in the backyard of 1222 S. Farmer Avenue. I tell the landlord of my profound attraction to Tempe & to this very spot.

8 Apr 08: Walking with a companion from north to south across Tempe Bridge. I recount to him the history of this bridge & the other bridges across the Salt River. I recall also the first time I walked the dry river bed beneath the bridge & saw hoboes seated on one of the arches, playing cards. I look forward to showing my companion the brass USGS benchmarks on the south side of the bridge.

23 May 08: We are walking south across 13th Street at S. Farmer Avenue, then reverse directions & walk north. And now, we are about to enter the alley that runs from 13th to 12th, between Farmer & Wilson, when to my left (west) I see a shallow stream of rippled water descending from a mound of brown earth & rock. We ascend the hillock to view the source of the stream, then descend & walk north along the alley with all its mysteries & memories.

30 May 08: Walking west on 10th Street at Maple Avenue, aware of my abiding longing to be here & of the many dreams of these streets I have had.

4 Jun 08: Residing in an apartment on Maple Avenue between 10th Street & University Drive. I must seek employment.

13 Jul 08: Looking for an apartment to rent on S. Farmer Avenue. At length, we see a "For Rent" sign. The owner is a Scot who informs us that the "toilet facilities" are shared among the apartments. This is discouraging but the rent is very reasonable & proximity to the ASU campus & the Hayden Library is also a favorable feature.
We walk the alley that runs from 13th to 12th between Farmer & Wilson. I have a notebook in my hand, taking notes on everything I see. I tell my companion that I have for many years had recurrent dreams of this location. This spot, I say, is for me the center of the earth.

4 Aug 08: There are only bare curbs & bare brown earth where houses once stood. To a companion, I lament the devastation, vent my sorrow & fury, calling down curses on the heads of the perpetrators. We walk 6th Street, 5th Street, Myrtle, Forest, east of Mill Avenue.

3 Sep 08: I am walking west on the north side of 13th Street, passing Maple & Ash Avenues. I intend to walk north along Ash, then south along Maple, viewing the houses I so admire. How this city takes hold of my emotions.

14 Oct 08: By great good fortune, we have returned to live in Tempe & found a rental among the apartments at 1214-1218 S. Farmer Avenue. I walk the front yard, the back yard, the passages between the buildings, thrilling to see all that I see, feeling a deep delight. And, I contemplate with pleasure all the things around me to which I am attracted: the side streets, the alleys, the r.r. tracks & trains, the ASU campus, the Hayden Library, bookshops, & more. One of my new neighbors asks me if I like it here. "I love every inch of this place," I reply.

2 Nov 08: It is night in Tempe & I am standing on the n.e. corner of 10th Street & Mill Avenue, looking west & anticipating with wonder & gladness the nostalgic pilgrimage that I will be undertaking in just a few minutes. I will cross Mill & walk west on 10th, turn south on Farmer & see again the Judd House & our old apartments. Though it is night, I am not afraid to walk these streets alone.

1 Jan 09: Walking south on Ash Avenue just south of 10th Street. Near 13th Street, I encounter 3 young women & inquire of them if they know of an artesian well nearby. They direct me across 13th to Tempe Junction. On the bare brown earth there just to the west of where the r.r. tracks meet (or divide) I see traces of an ancient Hohokam sculpture depicting a fertility spirit. And close by I see a narrow channel with water flowing in it. This is the natural spring I have been seeking.

13 Jan 09: I walk along the south side of 5th Street, east of Mill Avenue. I enter the Desert Flower Café.

30 Jan 09: Living again on S. Farmer Avenue (east side) just north of 13th Street. It is our first morning in our new apartment & we haven't a tea kettle or food. On the south side of 13th Street there are small fast food stands & as we study the menu someone passes leading a small elephant. Later, from the window of our apartment I see another person leading a small elephant. I appreciate the unexpected, unpredictable character of these events. I resolve henceforth to be attentive to every occurrence here, even the most commonplace & ordinary (such as the students walking on the other side of the street.) And now as rain begins to fall I stand near the n.w. corner of 13th & Farmer under an olive tree. To be in Tempe in the rain! I weep with the pain of my pleasure.

15 Feb 09: Tempe Center is soon to be torn down. I stand on that narrow strip of grass outside the supermarket between the asphalt parking lot & the cement sidewalk. I must take with me a small portion of this earth. And now I rush into Books Inc. in hope of finding a last book to purchase there. This is my last chance to be here, to see it. Soon all will be gone.

25 Apr 09: It is early morning as I approach Tempe Center from the north end (University Drive.) Customers are just beginning to arrive, parking their cars & entering the various stores. Today is the final day of a visit I have made to Tempe. I have seen the things I wanted to see, but I hope to have one last look at them today before departing. I walk

south along the cement sidewalk of Tempe Center, past the shops. From within one of the shops a radio is playing. I weep to think how much I will miss all of this.

7 Jun 09: Riding north in a car on University Drive with Tempe Center to my left (south.) I am sadly aware that the Center is to be razed. Later, walking north on Myrtle Avenue toward 6th Street.

11 Jun 09: Crossing Mill Avenue from east to west, intending to enter a shop.

14 Jul 09: Talking with a long-time resident of Tempe, I praise the blue sky above Tempe, tell of the powerful attraction I feel to the very earth here.

28 Jul 09: With two companions I climb the winding interior stairway of a three-story tower that stands north of 13th Street at Ash Avenue. The tower was built over a hundred years ago by an eccentric man & is currently for sale. We stand on the topmost floor looking out over Tempe, a magical view of the city. We descend. On the bottom floor, I see an old-fashioned cast iron wood-burning stove. I wonder how during my many walks through Tempe I can have missed this strange & prominent structure.

3 Aug 09: I stand on the north side of the Farmer-Goodwin House (820 S. Farmer Avenue.) Automobile parts & a clutter of oily mechanical articles are strewn on the lawn. I like the informality & unkempt character of the yard, it exemplifies the kind of unpretentious, slightly scruffy & dishevelled spirit that has always pleased me in Tempe. I recall long ago personal events connected with this mysterious house: summer nights, friends, reefer.

12 Oct 09: I thumb a ride with a family into Tempe. Disoriented in previously unknown 1890s quarter but at length I am on 13th Street at Roosevelt Avenue, walking east, & I am stirred & stimulated now as I am

approaching dear old Farmer Avenue. I recall all the times in the past when I came this way, walking to and from my dull job at the Jacques Cattell Press.

4 Mar 10: From E. 6th Street at Myrtle Avenue, I walk to the apartments at 1214-1218 S. Farmer Avenue. Now, I want to return to 6th Street, but my plan is to walk there by way of the alleys as much as possible. The idea of taking such a route has long appealed to me. It should be interesting.

12 Mar 10: A friend drives me east on University Drive. I want to see the apartments on S. Farmer Avenue, but somehow we miss the turn at Farmer, then Ash, then Maple. We turn right on Mill Avenue & as we approach 10th Street & the Dairy Queen I ask my friend to stop the car. I get out & stand gazing across Mill at Tempe Center, my heart full of joy to contemplate the quiet pleasures of the present and those still to come.

5 May 10: A nostalgic visit to the apartments at 1214-1218 S. Farmer Avenue. I walk the premises, looking at once familiar objects: the water heaters, the back doors, the electric meters, the wall enclosing the backyard. I chat with some of the current residents of the apartments, relating to them tales of wild & rowdy Parry's bar, cultivating marijuana plants here, backyard parties & gardens of long ago. I perceive, however, that no-one is interested.

30 May 10: Living once again in our former apartment at 1214 and a half S. Farmer Avenue. I go for a walk, south to 13th, turn right (west) then into the alley that runs from 13th to 12th between Wilson & Farmer Avenues. I am pervaded with a sense of the mystery of this place & with wonder at being here. I feel as if I could take flight here in the alley, soar above the streets & trees.

13 Jun 10: I sit in the Valley Art Theatre. In a few minutes the film will begin. In the half-dark, people are still arriving & finding seats. I'm here again & all is well. I'm here!

21 Jun 10: Walking south on Wilson Avenue, near 13th Street. I encounter two of my former students. I explain to them my deep attraction to Tempe, telling them that the most common motif in my dreams of Tempe is that of finding myself on a street & gazing about in fascination & joy, then weeping, overcome. In sympathy with my strange, sad confession, one of the students is moved to tears.

3 Jul 10: I enter Tempe on a bus, riding east on University Drive, turning left (north) on Mill Avenue, then right (east) on 5th Street. From the bus window I look out at the shops & houses. It affects me deeply. I feel myself on the verge of tears.

31 Jul 10: Walking south on the west side of S. Farmer Avenue, south of 13th Street. A wave of nostalgia engulfs me as I remember the many mornings I walked this way to work & the many afternoons when I returned homeward this way. Now, having nearly reached Broadway Road, I cross the street to walk north along the east side of the street.

4 Nov 10: I am elated & grateful to be walking in the alley that runs from 13th to 12th Street, between Wilson & Farmer Avenues. This is the center of the world. I look around with pleasure & interest: the stones, the garbage cans, the backyards, the sheds, the fences & trees.

21 Nov 10: I'm in the Valley Art Theatre! With companions, I sit watching a double feature: a crime-caper film & a Japanese noir. As we get up from our seats to leave the theatre, I turn to take in the décor. I want to cherish & memorize every detail of what I see. "I love this place," I remark to my companions, adding "I first came here in January of 1965." And now, we stand on the sidewalk in front of the Valley Art. Looking west into the night sky above the buildings I can see Orion.

30 Nov 10: Admiring the late summer flowers that are flourishing in the front yards of houses on 9th Street between Maple & Ash Avenues. My eyes dwell lovingly on the old houses. I must commit to memory all that I see.

16 Jan 11: There is an indentation about 30 inches wide in the asphalt near the n.w. corner of 13th Street & S. Farmer Avenue. With my shoe, I test the pliability of the depression. It is unfirm. I suspect that some subsurface movement has taken place. Now I turn my attention to the houses around me, drawn by their mystery. I must soon leave Tempe, though I don't want to depart.

3 Feb 11: I stroll Tempe Center then walk behind the Center, west of Myrtle Avenue. There are some cars parked there & a scruffy strip of earth & grass. I take in as much as I can perceive of what is before me. This time I will do everything slowly & deliberately. I begin by touching the sun-warm glass windshield of a parked car. This time I mean to stay here.

15 Feb 11: I stand at the western edge of the parking lot of Tempe Center, the n.w. corner, near Mill Avenue, not far from University Drive. I am anticipating a walk through the streets I love. In the distance, I see mountains. Now, however, I'm watching a clip from an old film or television series in which an automobile is travelling north along Mill Avenue. This is exciting! I can see the old buildings & shops, including a Sprouse-Reitz Store. I must find a copy of this film so that I can study the images more carefully.

25 Feb 11: From the north bank of the Salt River, I look toward Tempe Butte & the Hayden Flour Mill. I talk to strangers concerning the fate of Tempe Butte, whether or not it can be saved from the machinations of commercial developers & the (as ever) singularly ill-advised plans of the Tempe City Council. I have with me several documents pertinent to the dispute over the Butte, but I see that the strangers to whom I'm speaking are clearly indifferent to the issue.

26 Feb 11: Walking between Broadway Avenue & 13th Street on S. Farmer Avenue. I marvel to see the finely crafted houses & the lush vegetation & I feel upon me the exertion of the force-field, the magnetic current that draws me here.

9 Jul 11: Even as I conduct a tour of the ASU campus, I am fielding questions concerning locations on or near the campus. I inform one inquirer of the bookstore in the Memorial Union Building. I point out St. Mary's Church (Our Lady of Mount Carmel) & I indicate the Student Book Center across University Drive on the west side of College Avenue.

3 Sep 11: Standing with companions on the s.w. corner of the parking lot of Tempe Center. I relate to them tragic tales of old Tempe: the drunken, depressed man on a three day binge who accidentally shot a boy back in the 1890s, the Mexican bandits who robbed a grocery store on Mill Avenue, shooting a passerby on the street (the bullet still lodged in a palm tree on Mill Avenue.) Now, we walk 10th Street to S. Farmer Avenue. I swoon inwardly to see the houses, desperate with covetousness. I mention to my companions that for 30 years & more I have often dreamed of this street & this area. There is a commuter train full of students stuck at Farmer & 12th Street. And now, I am shocked & astounded to see that the buildings at 1218 S. Farmer Avenue have been levelled. Apart from dirt & debris nothing remains. The outline of the walls & rooms is still visible on the bare earth. I weep with grief. All is gone. I'm stunned, stricken.

19 Oct 11: Excitement & amazement within my spirit as I walk the east side of Mill Avenue, passing Laird & Dines, then turning right (east.) I walk east on the south side of 5th Street. I wonder if I have time to walk to the old apartments at 1214-1218 S. Farmer Avenue.

28 Feb 12: My visit to Tempe will very soon be at an end. I stand in the front yard of 1218 S. Farmer, closely examining every object in my field of vision, touching leaves, tree trunks, bending to touch plants. Perceiving my attentive interest in commonplace things, one of the residents of the

apartments asks me: are you very attracted to this place? "Yes," I reply, "unfortunately I am."

6 Mar 12: I'm walking west on the south side of 10th Street, past Ash Avenue, approaching the r.r. tracks. Looking about me at the houses I so admire, I am struck with the near perfection of this moment & swept with a wave of painful joy.

10 Jul 12: It's early morning & I'm walking north on the east side of Mill Avenue between 6th & 5th Streets. I thrill in my spirit to pass on my right the wonderful Valley Art Theatre. I remember other occasions when I have stood just here. I must cross the street & hurry along to my job. I seem always to be rushed. But even so I can sense the romance of Tempe. I feel still my deep attachment to this place.

8 Sep 12: Overhead are the stars as I walk north on the east side of S. Farmer Avenue to 10th Street.

8 Nov 12: I stand in wonder & joy on the north side of the street at the intersection of 10th Street & Ash Avenue. *It's 10th Street!* Mythic, magic, enchanted 10th Street! I weep to be here & oh that little house in which I have always wanted to live!

7 Dec 12: Together with two affluent businessmen, I look at an old brick house on the west side of College Avenue at 7th Street. One of the businessmen reckons that the house has too much exposure to the sun & would be uncomfortably hot in the summer. I explain that for me the ideal residence in Tempe is one from which I can walk every morning to the Hayden Library to read the newspapers & magazines. Now, we take a short journey & stand before an old building which one of the businessmen intends to use or sell. I realize that it is Hicks Machine Company (24 W. 7th Street.) With a thrill of excitement I begin to inspect every detail of the construction, touching the brick walls, stooping to the ground to scrutinize features. Behind the building, I

discover a white stone tablet inscribed with black letters. I have never before seen anything like this & feel pleased & intrigued.

28 Dec 12: With a group of my students, I enter marvellous old Parry's bar on Mill Avenue. We sit together at a round wooden table. I recount tales of former years & times in Parry's: the boisterous, rowdy saloon atmosphere, the fertile craziness, the shots fired into the ceiling, the oldtimers playing cards on Sunday afternoons, the sense of connection with the past. I note with some chagrin that my intense attachment to this place is not shared by my companions. They are only very slightly amused to hear of the historical associations & the wild vitality of the place. I understand that Parry's will soon be sold. I fear for the future of this unique shrine.

6 Feb 13: After long absence, I have returned to live in the apartments at 1214-1218 S. Farmer Avenue. I perceive that some changes have been made to doors & windows but the alterations are acceptable. Some old friends are living there still. I am happy to have returned & eager to explore the grounds, surroundings & the neighborhood.

31 Mar 13: Standing on a sidewalk on S. Farmer Avenue, I realize with delight that the city extends around me in every direction. It's all there & I can go anywhere & see the things I cherish.

15 Apr 13: I'm studying an old Tempe tourist brochure from the 1930s. There are photos of Tempe Beach & a notice of the opening hours of the swimming pool. At the bottom of one page there is a rough hand-drawn map of the city, showing Tempe Butte & the downtown streets. The names of ndividual shops & restaurants are indicated. I am very keen to learn what is said in the brochure about Parry's bar.

23 May 13: An early Saturday morning in Tempe as I walk with a companion on the east side of Mill Avenue, just south of Tempe Bridge. The shops are not yet open. I note large flat areas where old buildings

have been knocked down. The downtown has been maimed, mutilated. I feel dismay & disgust with the hubristic folly of it all.

31 May 13: Only sad scattered remnants endure of the old houses I knew here on E. 6th Street near Collage Avenue. Nearly all that was original & quaint, all that was vivid & endearing is gone. I grieve to see that the relentless homogenisation of everything continues apace.

11 Jan 14: Walking along the north side of 10th Street, west of Mill Avenue. As we approach Ash Avenue I look to my left (south) & see a gray mist in the air, a slight haze. I call attention to this mysterious phenomenon & we cross the street to take photographs of it. I am reminded of a hot, humid summer's day once long ago when I witnessed something similar: the loud whining of cicadas in tall old trees & a light mist in the air.

14 Mar 14: Glad & alert, I walk north along the west side of College Avenue, north of University Drive. I walk past Campus Drugs & the book stores. A new multi-story building has been constructed on the east side of the street. I note that it is occupied by offices of doctors & lawyers & by municipal bureaus.

16 Mar 14: In the alley that runs from 13th to 12th Street between Wilson & Farmer Avenues, I search the ground hoping to discover some memento or artefact or even a stone to take away with me. Many of the bare earthen areas along the borders of the alley have now been paved with asphalt or cement. In conversation with a stranger, I remark: "you can't know how many times I have dreamed of this alley. I've dreamed of it for over 30 years."

20 Apr 14: Walking with companions through the alley (12th to 13th, between Wilson & Farmer.) Passing the west (rear) end of the 1214 and a half building, I see that many of the windows of the building have been broken. I note also a ladder leaning against the back of the building. I am informed by a companion that the broken windows are a measure

undertaken in revenge by a tribe of outcasts who subscribe to a superstitious belief that ladders should be made available to them. Accordingly, if owners or occupants don't provide an accessible ladder, the windows are broken. I reflect that I have long desired to climb to the flat rooftop of 1214 and a half to view from there the surrounding streets & trees & to recline there on a summer night under the stars.

12 May 14: Together with a companion, I call on an acquaintance of his. As we knock on the door of his apartment, I realize that this is 1214 and a half S. Farmer Avenue, No. 1, an apartment that B. & I rented 1969 – 1970. The door is opened & my companion & I enter. Carefully & intensely, I examine the intereior. I am utterly amazed & deeply affected to stand here again. I relate to the resident & my companion comic stories of past events that took place here. I also confess that in my psyche this is the center of the world, "this is my true address." I mention, too, my many night-dreams of this area. And now, to cap my joy, we call upon the resident of 1218 S. Farmer Avenue, no. 3. I am permitted to enter the apartment. Again, with profound pleasure I scrutinize every detail of the interior. And again, I mention to the current resident my numerous night-dreams of this place. And now my dreams have come true!

20 Jun 14: Admiring the houses on both sides of the street, we walk the Wilson/Farmer & Maple/Ash streets between 13th Street & 10th Street.

10 Jul 14: Walking along the east side of Mill Avenue at the 400 block. The old territorial buildings of the downtown are boarded up. To my companion I remark how very dear these buildings are to me. Given the ongoing displacement of the past with bland standardization, I fear for their future.

26 Oct 14: Having walked north on the east side of S. Farmer Avenue, I turn right (east) on 10th Street. I feel attraction, yearning & such sorrow that I choke & weep. I know that I can never return to live here. It is

impossible. And yet I am drawn here by a powerful attachment. Now, I will continue east, across Mill Avenue, to the ASU campus.

19 Dec 14: I'm standing at the intersection of 13th Street & Ash Avenue, savouring the prospect of a leisurely stroll north along Ash. And now, as I walk, I come to a grassy vacant lot with a "For Sale" sign planted in the ground. I am eager to stand somewhere where I have never before set foot so I walk onto the lot, onto virgin territory of old Tempe.

23 Feb 15: Walking north with companions along the west side of Mill Avenue at 6th Street. I am pleased by the shops we pass. And now at the former site of the late, lamented Parry's bar, I discourse upon the unique virtues of that venerable old saloon. Gone now, erased & replaced by the insipid & the nondescript. The dullards have swept all before them.

18 Apr 15: Feeling again that mysterious kinship with this space, these streets, I stroll with a companion from S. Farmer Avenue onto 13th Street then west to Wilson Avenue, turning north there.

23 Jun 15: An acquaintance tells me tales of murder & death associated with Tempe Butte as we pass it on our left (having walked into Tempe from the north.) The stories that he relates all took place in the late 19th & early 20th century. Now, my acquaintance shows me a hidden courtyard behind the 400 block on the east side of Mill Avenue. Immediately, I feel wonder & a thrilling current of mystery. The courtyard is uneven bare dirt with a few scattered rocks. This is a remnant of the original Tempe, the early days!

24 Oct 15: Walking north on the west side of Mill Avenue at 5th Street. I tell my companion of my profound & powerful attraction to Tempe.

8 Nov 15: In a fraternity house somewhere south of Apache Boulevard, I deliver a lecture on the spirit of Tempe as I experienced it: the lingering vestiges of the past, the bohemian flavor, a place of refuge for the authentic & the quirky, the individual & the idiosyncratic. Later, I rake

leaves in a garden & gazing across a backyard fence into the garden of an old house I see there mysterious bas-reliefs, probably dating from the 1920s.

18 Dec 15: Riding north on Mill Avenue in a car with companions. Passing 10th Street & continuing north, I look west at the houses on Mill, including the one in which my dentist had his practice. I study the porches, pillars, doors & windows, all the endearing particulars. I am at once heartened & hurt to see these things.

20 Dec 15: We are living on the north side of E. 6th Street between Myrtle Avenue & Forest Avenue. I discover nearby the remnants of an old orchard, a vestige of old Tempe that thrills me.

We walk east on E. 6th Street passing to our right (south) the remnants of the VFW Hall, walking beneath the arches. I am relieved that these at least remain. I tell my companion of a brief visit I made to this street years ago when I stood stunned & absolutely amazed to be here. How unreal & dreamlike it seemed to me then.

6 May 16: I pass on my right (east) the Social Sciences Building on the ASU campus, remembering with sadness the many walks I took along Orange Mall long ago with my dear dog. At the same time, I feel within me a tingling sensation of glad anticipation in thinking that I can now repeat this walk many times, as often as I like. To my left I see the stone & cement planters & benches. All is as it was long ago. And now I am approaching the Language & Literature Building of dear memory.

22 Jul 16: A happy walk north along S. Farmer Avenue. We have returned to live in the apartments at 1214-1218.

31 Aug 16: With an old friend who lived in Tempe in the mid-Sixties, I walk 10th Street, Maple & Ash Avenues. I remind him that I visited him here in Tempe on two occasions: once on 9th Street & once on 13th

Street. Mysterious residences those were, redolent of psychedelic mysticism.

24 Sep 16: Watching a Hollywood fiction film on television, I am greatly & pleasantly amazed to see scenes in which appear exterior views of the 1218 S. Farmer Avenue apartments.

7 Oct 16: There is a film on television that is set in Tempe in the 1920s. I recognize the territorial buildings & 6th Street. Exciting to see.

22 Dec 16: Evening is falling & we have just completed moving our belongings into an apartment at 1218 S. Farmer Avenue. Wanting to have a look at the stars, I walk past the front yard & onto the sidewalk. I reflect how glad & grateful I am to be here.

24 Dec 16: Suddenly, inexplicably, I am standing in front of the Judd House at 1208 S. Farmer Avenue! My heart soars to see it & to see again the old apartments next door to the south. Perhaps somehow I can contrive to gain entry into the Judd House. I would so like to see the interior. I would also like to see again the interiors of the apartments next door where we lived long ago. How pleasantly strange that would be.

27 Jan 17: Walking south on the west side of Mill Avenue, passing Tempe Beach Park on my right (west.) Many memories, some going back to 1958 (5th grade "ditch day.") All my particles accelerate in anticipation of seeing again the mysterious old Casa Loma & the former site of celebrated & storied Parry's bar. I can browse in Changing Hands Books at 414 Mill Avenue.

25 Feb 17: Walking north with companions on west side of Ash Avenue to where it intersects with 10th Street. I stop to gaze wistfully at one of the houses there that has ever attracted & allured me. I explain to my companions that this is one of the houses in which I have always longed to live. And now, turning west we come to the r.r. tracks. I search the

weedy area along the side of the tracks for a discarded old rusty r.r. spike to take away as a memento of Tempe (one that has endured the blazing heat of the summer sun & felt the rain & known the cold of winter nights, one coated with the earth of Tempe.) I find one: rusty, bent, soiled. Just the thing. To my companions, I recount my affection for the freight trains that roll along these tracks, rumbling & with whistles moaning: box cars, flat cars, tank cars, gondolas, even red cabooses.

17 Mar 17: On the first day of a brief two-day visit to Tempe, I stand at the intersection of S. Farmer Avenue & 10th Street. I can look north & south along the length of Farmer & I can look east along the length of 10th Street. It is so poignant, so soul-piercing to see it. Aloud, I cry: "Oh my Farmer! Oh my 10th Street! Oh my Farmer! Oh my 10th Street!" My cry is at once one of joy & of sorrow, the woe of deep yearning & the knowledge of all the years that this has been here just as it is while I have been far away. All the lost years & even now I can't remain here. I survey, I gaze, I study, I examine & inspect all that I see.

29 Mar 17: We walk E. 6th Street, turn south on Forest & walk to University Drive. And now we will have a last look at the Congregational Church at the corner of 6th & Myrtle which we have learned is slated for destruction by developers.

6 May 17: Happy psychic rapport with old Tempe: trees, alleys, remnants of the past. On Ash Avenue north of 13th Street I come upon an old wooden schoolhouse. The building is to be sold. The developer-buyer stands looking at it. "I suppose you intend to build a highrise here," I comment. And now near 9th Street & Maple a large old tree has been felled by dendrochologists from ASU. The many interior rings of the tree – so long hidden & secret – are now exposed. I think of all the years, the seasons, weathers, human events, the times I lived here, all encoded in the tree rings.

1 Sep 17: To a group of European visitors to Tempe (considering retirement or winter homes there) I extol the advantages of the city: a university town with a huge library, cultural activities, plays, musical performances at Grady Gammage, an art cinema, a walkable downtown with restaurants & cafés.
Walking west we stroll the north side of 13th to S. Farmer Avenue.

13 Sep 17: Returning home to 1218 S. Farmer Avenue no. 3 after a day of work. It is raining lightly & the earth is wet. I approach our apartment by way of the alley. As I turn my key in the front door, I think to myself: *this is where I want to be.*

13 Dec 17: Staring with admiration at an old house at 9th Street & Maple Avenue. It is empty, slated to be torn down. I speculate on the lives of the early inhabitants of the house. I wonder whether any incidental artefacts will be found beneath the floorboards or elsewhere in the house.

10 Jan 18: As I walk west past the Memorial Union building on the ASU campus, I recall working long ago in the bookstore that was located here. I remember, too, the many occasions on which I bought books here. I look through the windows into the space where the bookstore was located at that time & see that there are metal shelves & stacks of books within. Apparently, the bookstore is soon to be re-established here. I will return when it opens. And now, I walk north along Orange Mall, past the fountain, past the Hayden Library.

5 Feb 18: It is afternoon on Mill Avenue. We enter the Valley Art Theatre, walk through the lobby into the seating area where renovations are taking place. The carpeting has been removed, exposing wooden floor boards. Busy workmen stand on scaffolding or stand hammering, drilling or painting. I approach the owner, Mr. Harkins, introducing myself & explaining my strong affection for the Valley Art Theatre, my long-standing yearning just to stand here in this space. "For me, this is sacred ground," I say.

7 Feb 18: I have returned to Tempe for a brief visit. I walk north along the sidewalk of Mill Avenue (on the east side of the street at 3rd Street.) I reflect that I must use my few days here to the fullest advantage. I must have no cause to reproach myself in time to come for not having seen as much as I could have done.

10 Feb 18: We walk south on the west side of Mill Avenue at 4th Street. We cross Mill at 6th & walk east. A large luxury hotel & bland condos have supplanted the neighborhood we used to know.

13 Mar 18: We enter the seating area of the Valley Art Theatre. It is afternoon & no film is being shown, but behind a curtain on the stage an organist is practicing. I look at every detail of the interior: ceiling, carpet, seats, lamps, wooden stage, screen, curtains.

18 Apr 18: We have taken residence again in our former apartment at 1214 and a half S. Farmer Avenue. Our guests stand drinking & talking both inside the apartment & on the open space between our building & the front building. This is where I stood, I remember, hanging clothes on the clothes line, the mild October evening after I had read in *The Phoenix Gazette* of Jack Kerouac's death.

26 Jun 18: I approach from the south the intersection of 10th Street & S. Farmer Avenue. I groan with woe to see that 10th Street has been widened into a boulevard & that many of the houses so dear to me have been demolished.

2 Sep 18: From the n.w. corner of Mill Avenue & 10th Street, I walk west, turning right (north) on Maple Avenue. I observe the autumn leaves on the trees: yellow, red, orange. When I reach University Avenue, I turn right (east) then right again (south) on Mill Avenue, return to 10th Street.

14 Oct 18: In warm sunlight I walk along the west side of S. Farmer Avenue, pausing on the sidewalk in front of an old house where the

owner has stacked items to be picked up by the city waste services. I rummage among the items, salvaging some partly used spiral notebooks. A young woman emerges from the house, confirms that she is disposing of the items & is happy that they can be of use to me.

5 Nov 18: Interesting, attractive shops on Mill Avenue as my bus passes from north to south, then a ride along S. Farmer Avenue & University Drive. I resolve to walk these streets later: 10th, Maple, Ash. The appeal, the allure of the city is still strong.

12 Nov 18: 5th Street, east of Mill Avenue. Then driven south on Mill. As the car stops for the traffic light at University, I ask the driver to pull into the parking lot of Tempe Center. I have suddenly realized that we could see 1214 & 1218 S. Farmer Avenue again. I explain to the driver that that location is for me "sacred space." I have dreamed of it numerous times. Moreover, it is unlikely that I will ever again have a chance to see it. The driver is agreeable to my wishes & we set off. I give directions where to turn. In a few minutes I will be there again. It's unbelievable!

5 Dec 18: My visit to Tempe is limited to just a few days. With a companion, I walk north on the west side of Mill Avenue, between 13th & 10th. My companion expresses a preference to walk on the other side of Mill, but I insist that we remain where we are, explaining my attachment to 10th Street, a street so very dear to me.

10 Dec 18: I sense the mystery of the place, feel a tingling excitement in my body, feel the pull of Tempe as I stand on the east side of S. Farmer Avenue near University Drive. I walk south, thrilled & fascinated by every house. Ah, 10th Street! And now, east on 10th to Mill Avenue. I inspect the bare, vacant space where the Diary Queen once stood. How sad & how unnecessary that it is gone. Oh, oh, how I wish I could have had a career here in Tempe, taught at ASU, known the place & the weathers every day.

14 Dec 18: Admiring the few old houses remaining at 6th Street & Forest
Avenue. I fear, though, that they are doomed to be razed. I look forward
to walking 7th Street, Myrtle Avenue, College Avenue.

2 Apr 19: Walking with a companion along the east side of S. Farmer
Avenue, nearing 9th Street. I express my admiration for the Chavez
House at 927 S. Farmer Avenue. The shingle roof, the pillared porch, the
humble, handsome appearance of this old adobe house. I would so have
liked to live here. We proceed to University Drive, turn right (east.)
Near the intersection is a vacant lot of brown dirt and weeds. I mention
to my companion that such lots are to me like the last fragments of
frontier Tempe, small unsettled areas like little oases amid the ever
more slick and shiny cityscape.

4 Jul 19: Driven in a car by an acquaintance, I direct the driver from our
position at 6th Street & S. Farmer Avenue south to University Drive, east
& south onto Mill Avenue, & finally to the s.w. corner of Mill & 10th
Street, where I get out. And now, rain is falling.

15 Jul 19: I am walking east on the north side of University Drive
between Forest & College Avenues. I savour the prospect of turning
north on College & revisiting sites sacred to my life. I am at once
exhilarated & downcast, so glad to be here yet feeling keenly the
poignance of my loss.

15 Sep 19: Seated at a table with two companions, one of whom is
looking to find an apartment for his college-bound daughter. He
mentions that he has seen an ad for a rental apartment at 1141 S. Farmer
Avenue but – not being at all acquainted with the city – is unsure
whether the location is a good one. I am excited to hear Farmer Avenue
mentioned & begin to hope ardently that we will drive there to have a
look at the apartment so that I will be able to see again all the dear
landmarks of my past. I mention some of the advantages of that address,
hoping my remarks will inspire an inspection of the apartment at that
address.

29 Nov 19: Living again at 1214 S. Farmer Avenue. Our dinner guest arrives: Nick Nolte.

4 Dec 19: As I walk enraptured along the north side of 10th Street, between Maple & Ash Avenues, I speak to a companion of my abiding & intense attraction to Tempe, to this very space on the earth. For years I have yearned to be just here, I say. We cross the r.r. tracks & turn left (south) on S. Farmer Avenue.

14 Dec 19: With sudden joyous amazement, I realize that I am on 10th Street! (The north side of the street, just east of the r.r. tracks.) I'm walking east toward Mill Avenue. I rejoice in my spirit & relish every detail my eyes survey: the parked cars, the plastic trash bins, the houses, the bushes, the trees, the curbs, the asphalt, the earth.

31 Dec 19: I'm standing in what once was Rundle's Market but the interior has been radically re-modelled & the store re-named. Even the counter has been relocated & the wonderful ornate old cash register is gone. To the woman clerk behind the counter, I recount the glories of the original Rundle's: the wide selection of magazines including *The Atlantic, Esquire, The Saturday Review* and *Harper's,* a rotating wire book rack of paperback books, the shelves of canned goods, the oldfashioned beer cooler & more. The woman informs me that the city council plans to raze the building.

11 Feb 20: Alert, vividly aware, I walk behind the buildings between 6th Street & 5th Street on the east side of Mill Avenue. And then, I'm walking on the east side of S. Farmer Avenue near 13th Street. To live here I am willing to live in a tree. I will select one in which to take up residence.

Tempe, Tempe, nur du allein
sollst stets die Stadt
meiner Traüme sein!

APPENDIX I

From the Burning

"everything is burning"

Additapariyaya Sutta

The Chinese-owned cantina was the only two story building in the village. The street was rutted, a dog was barking. Thin blue coils of mesquite smoke rose into the late afternoon sun and hung over the adobe houses. My horse was tender footed, having cast a shoe the day before. I drew rein in front of the cantina, uncinched my saddle and turned my horse into the corral.

Inside the cantina it was dim and chill. The floor was bare earth, sprinkled and swept clean, but there was a lingering odor of stale tobacco and spilled liquor. A pool table occupied the center of the room. A tarnished mirror was nailed to one wall; a clock and a calendar were hung on the wall behind the counter where a shelf held canned goods and bottles.

I set my watch by the clock on the wall, paid in advance for one night, took my key from the Chinaman and climbed the stairs to the room. On the window hung a discolored linen curtain. Rags, newspapers and flattened cans had been used to plug the cracks between the boards. There was a table, a lamp and a basin. Down the hallway, in another room, a man was coughing.

There was a wedding dance in the village until late that night. Then the rain came quick and hard, and wind seething in the trees. I slept and awoke suddenly in the dark, wondering where I was. Outside there was gunfire and shouting. I rose and dressed quickly, pulling on my boots and putting on my hat. In the intervals between the sharp reports of firearms I could hear the ticking of my watch. *Por Dios!* someone cried.

Heavy steps ascended the stairs from the cantina and thumped down the hallway. There was the sharp crack of a gunshot nearby and then another shot was fired and a man grunted in pain. I heard someone fall to the floor. My heart was beating hard and my breath came fast. Panting and shaking, I cocked my .44 drawing back the hammer slowly, easing the catching of the sear with a steady pressure of the thumb. Outside it was getting light. I moved away from the window to the darkest corner of the room and stood facing the door.

From the street below there was the sound of gunfire and of horses neighing frantically. Then there was a deafening report and sparks and splinters flew into the room. My ears rang and vivid colors drifted before my eyes. The door opened, struck the wall, then half closed again. A man entered and as though we were two separate wheels rotating in opposite directions we stood facing each other. Blue-white flashes flared from his pistol and I felt the concussion and the heat before I heard the roar. A bullet passed between my arm and my left side, just grazing my ribs above the heart and tearing off most of my jacket and shirt.

I fired once and then fired again and the man jack-knifed backward out of the room as if a mule had kicked him in the chest. Then moments later he staggered back into the room, gasping, his arms hanging at his sides. He looked at me; our eyes met. He was smiling faintly. Colored filaments still whirled before my eyes. I started to shake uncontrollably. He lifted his pistol and held it before his face gazing at it as if he did not know the use of such an object. Then his smile faded and he knelt heavily and then fell forward to the floor and lay face down and did not move.

I stood still for a long time holding my .44 at my side and very slowly the light in the room grew brighter. Except for the crowing of cocks and the chatter of birds there was silence. My left side burned where the bullet had grazed me. I felt weak and a little strange as if I were remembering something that had happened to me a long time ago or as if for an instant I had remembered who I was and had then forgotten again.

As the room grew lighter I could see that the dead man on the floor was dressed in the uniform of a *rurale* in dark-gray whipcord with black braid down the legs of his trousers. Outside the door in the hallway lay his sombrero with a silver eagle-and-snake insignia.

I stepped over the dead man and walked down the corridor. In a room at the end of the hallway there was another dead man, dressed only in long underwear, an American by the look of him. He had been shot through the chest and he lay face-up on the floor in a large dark pool of blood. His blue eyes were open, his mouth smiling a little; tobacco-brown teeth showing. On the table lay his Dunlap hat. He had hung his shirt and jacket over a chair before going to bed. Painfully, I removed my own torn jacket and shirt and put on those of the dead man.

Carrying my saddle bags in my left hand and my .44 in my right, I descended the stairs to the cantina. There was no-one there. I stepped through the rear doorway and onto the patio and stood in the cold morning sunlight. Jerked meat and peppers hung along the walls and above the door. I pulled down handfuls and put them into the pockets of my new jacket. I began to chew a piece of jerky. I entered the doorway again and walked through the cantina. There was no sign of the Chinaman.

I stepped into the street. It was muddy and puddled with the night's rain and there were deep tracks of many horses. Apart from the grunting of pigs, the bleating of goats and the clucking of chickens, the village was silent. No smoke rose from the adobe houses. The corral beside the cantina was empty, the gate open; the horses had been driven off. Down the muddy street a goat was eating a straw sombrero. I stood shivering in the chill sunlight. My head ached fiercely and felt empty and dry.

I returned to the cantina and from the shelf behind the counter I took a can of sardines, a can of fruit and a box of crackers. I ate and then I poured myself a shot of *aguardiente* and rolled a smoke and tried to think what to do. I had pretty much made up my mind to start walking back to Ojo Frederico where I knew I could buy a mount when I heard and felt the thud of approaching hooves. I took my .44 from my belt and went out the backdoor of the cantina just as a riderless, saddleless gray horse, reins trailing, entered the open adobe corral and then stood drinking at the stone trough. The gray was streaked with dust and dried lather, his mane and tail matted with burrs. I let him drink then put a nosebag of grain on him and rubbed him down.

I headed north but I had not ridden for more than an hour when I heard the sound of approaching horses. I reined in, dismounted and led the gray to a grove of mesquite trees. A party of twenty Carranzistas passed along the road, headed south. They rode in columns of twos with a rider at the end of the column leading a pack mule with a machine gun. After that I kept off the roads, riding narrow trails through dense scrub and thorn and cactus, down dry washes, and through sandy arroyos. The white glare of the sun made my head ache and my left side smarted where the bullet had grazed me.

In the inside pocket of the dead man's coat I found two creased colored postcards that he had written. One of the cards was a picture of the Juzgado De Letras – the jail – in Juarez, Mexico. The card was addressed to Mrs. Emily P. Davis, 19 Birch Street, New Rochelle, New York, U.S.A. At the upper left hand of the card the man had written "Ciudad Juarez, Mexico, October 24, 1915." The message on the card read: "Dear Ma, This is a picturesque but dirty town. At the Rio Grande – a miserable little dried up river – I saw people living in thatch and grass huts. It is very hot and dusty. El Paso runs into this town. Affectionately, Albert."

The other card depicted adobe houses and a mill with a water wheel on the banks of the Rio Grande.

The card was addressed to Miss Emily G. Davis at the same address and was dated the same day. The message on the card read: "Dear Emmie, At the American side a U.S. Customs Officer made the passengers stand while he searched them and on the Mexican side a Mexican official went through the car and searched us with his eyes. The people are very dark but wear tall broad rimmed hats and some of them shawls though it is very hot. Affectionately, Albert."

There were no postage stamps on the cards. That was probably why he had not posted them. He had carried them with him in his pocket for months.

I had not read anything in English for a long time. I read the cards many times over and then replaced them in the inside pocket of the coat. Miss Emmie Davis would be Albert's kid sister, I thought. I wondered how old Emmie was and how long she would live. If she was fifteen or sixteen now, she might live until 1975 or 1980. She would never know what happened to her older brother. When she died Albert would be forgotten.

I crossed the line at Pena Blanca wash a few miles west of Nogales. There was about three inches of clear water running over sand and rock in the bottom of the wash and I dismounted to let my horse drink and to take a drink myself and fill my canteen. I knelt and drank deeply of the rippling water and then I spied a dead range cow lying upstream. For an antiseptic I took a chew of my cigarette tobacco. I approached and saw that the cow had been partly skinned and sandals cut out of the hide. Probably Yaquis, I thought. They were known to use this route to smuggle firearms and ammunition into Mexico.

I was still several days' ride from Tempe. I did not know what it was that made me feel impelled to return there. The urge to go there had grown upon me and I had long known that that was where I was headed.

I rode into Tempe across the new bridge over the Salt River. It was a fine bridge and would last a long time. It was built mostly by convict labor recruited from the territorial prison at Florence. I probably knew some of the men who had built it. I left my horse at Buck's livery stable and took a room at the Casa Loma Hotel. In my room I reclined on the bed smoking and studying faint discolorations on the ceiling and then I looked out the window at the street, the mill and the butte. On the windowsill there was a fine black dust, four burnt matches, a dead moth. My mind seemed full of distances. I wondered if the sun had addled me. I did not know why I had come here.

That night I dreamed of fire burning and awoke in the dark with a start and my heart pounding. Then I slept again and woke at cockcrow. Daylight came gray through the window. I thought I saw a spider moving slowly across the white ceiling but the more I looked at it the less it was there. I rose and dressed, rolled a smoke and stood smoking at the open window watching the sun rise on the other side of the butte. I could hear the sound of a windmill squealing as it turned in the light dawn breeze. I breakfasted in the hotel restaurant among half a dozen commercial travellers. I listened with interest to the fragments of conversation from the nearby tables: "he took a bottle and swallowed till he was fool drunk," ... "it ain't often I misjudge men," ..."got killed by a Mex name of José Gonzales." No one spoke to me. As always, as everywhere, I was a stranger, an observer.

I set my watch by the hotel clock and then I walked over to Mexican town to look up old Chiang Li. His grocery store was boarded up. There was a little Mexican girl skipping rope nearby and I asked her if she knew what had happened to Chiang Li. She told me Chiang Li had hanged himself in his shop during the week between Christmas and the New Year. Everyone in the neighborhood had been very shocked, she said. Since then she had been afraid to go near the shop. She said that *espantos* – ghosts – came out of the chimney at night because the Chinaman had buried a treasure there. At night, she said, you could see the ghosts floating above the house.

In the bright late morning I walked south and west out of the town, following a dirt road just west of the railroad tracks. I walked about a mile or so in chill winter sunlight thinking how this world need never have happened. In a weedy brown field west of the road I saw a chair standing level on the dry, light brown earth. It was a wooden, rush-bottomed chair, the round legs charred, as if it had been rescued from a burning house.

With a sense of purpose I walked back to Mill Street. In the general merchandise store I bought a spade and then returned with it to the field where the chair stood. All afternoon in the winter sun I dug in the dry earth to a depth of about five feet. I was glad that no-one saw me digging there. I placed the chair upright at the bottom of the hole. I did not want to bury it so deep that it would not someday be found. There would be about 20 inches of dirt between the top of the back of the chair and the surface of the earth.

In the fading light I filled the hole and tamped it with the back of the shovel and tramped on it, walking back and forth across it until the soil felt hard and solid under my feet. The light was dim now. The air was growing chill. There was a faint smell of pinon woodsmoke. I dropped the spade from my hand and stood atop the filled hole and took my watch from my pocket. In the red dusk I could still read the dark hands against the white clock face. It was 6:32 p.m. The day was February the 17th, 1916. From this hour and this place invisible lines radiated in every direction across the earth and the sky and through time.

APPENDIX II

Unreal City: The Ravaging of Tempe

"Place is the only reality,
 the true core of the universal."
William Carlos Williams

"A new daimon has got into the world,
 a daimon that cancels place ..."
Guy Davenport

It can at times be difficult to believe that there does not somewhere exist a powerful, perverse, sinister, secret organization whose purpose is the eradication from the earth of all manifestations of individuality, authenticity, originality and human meaning. Certainly, there is considerable inferential evidence to suggest the operation of such a conspiracy – a clandestine Society for the Propagation of Insipidity, or League for the Disenchantment of the World – an evil cabal relentlessly scheming and intriguing, acting in the shadows, co-ordinating a network of agents, with the aim of establishing for its colorless, cold-blooded membership a homogeneous world habitat of standardized banality.

The black irony is that were there such a fiendish plot it could scarcely have been more brilliantly successful, more spectacularly effective in achieving its goals than the loose, obtuse affiliation of city councils and city planners, architects and developers that have reduced the city of Tempe to a wilderness of blandness.

Year to year, Tempe continues to grow larger and larger, and yet year by year there is less and less of it – less of the real city, the true Tempe. About 90% of what once – only recently – made Tempe a charming, distinctive, attractive city has been eradicated. Only a few forlorn fragments of the original city yet remain, together with the last leafy, graceful neighborhood.

In order to appreciate the scale of the destruction of Tempe and the character of the cultural loss that is the result of that destruction, you must first have a sense of what Tempe was before the process of "urban renewal" was begun in the late 1970s, culminating in the 1990s.

Once, amid the endless, anonymous suburbs, the desolate similitude, stultifying blandness and commercial squalor of Phoenix and the pseudo-quaintness of Scottsdale (known locally then as "the west's most phoney town"), Tempe was an oasis of the authentic, the local, and the individual. Until the wholesale razing of buildings and entire neighborhoods began, the old, original town of Tempe was still virtually intact. From Tempe Bridge to University Avenue, Mill Avenue consisted of block after block of territorial buildings, interspersed with a few newer structures, and on the side streets of the old downtown there were also many historic buildings. To the east and west of Mill Avenue there were wonderful old neighborhoods with houses in a variety of architectural styles, some dating from the late 19th or early 20th centuries, others built in the 1920s and 30s. There were mansions and bungalows side by side, houses built of brick, wood, stucco and adobe, each house with a physiognomy of its own, a character of its own. There were tall old trees and luxuriant gardens. The flavor of history, the romance of the past still lingered in those streets.

These districts possessed both quiet dignity and quirky charm. There was much to draw the eye. There was a richness of tone and texture, a sense of temporal depth, a sort of aura or resonance, and a kind of mystery to these old neighborhoods. Walking the historic WPA sidewalks, you noticed the subjective accent of each house, its picturesque simplicity or fine architectural detail. To walk there was gratifying, satisfying; you paused to note and admire, to gaze and savour. You came upon fig trees and pomegranate bushes, prickly pear and palm trees, agave and barrel cactus, hibiscus and bougainvillea, olive and lemon and orange trees, tamarisk, cottonwood, eucalyptus and oleander, mistletoe growing on maple trees. You encountered hummingbirds, met the occasional lizard, heard cicadas and mourning doves in the trees. One component of attraction in these districts was their intermittently almost rustic or rural character, with spacious yards and large vacant lots overgrown with wild grasses and weeds. In spite of the usual grid of streets, there seemed something idiosyncratic and asymmetrical to these neighborhoods; there was a pleasant oddness, a rich, irregular mix of things that had built itself up organically over the decades. Beauty and character had accrued there slowly. There was diversity and contrast, historical layering, and the patina of time upon things.

With the exception of a few vestiges, all of this is gone now. All that now remains of charm in Tempe are the few scattered surviving buildings on Mill Avenue, here and there an old church, and the Maple, Ash and Farmer area between University Avenue and 13th Street, and that excellent neighborhood is constantly under siege, continually menaced by developers who have already made and continue to make destructive incursions there, spoiling the harmony and tone of the whole, devouring the neighborhood by increments.

Of the real Tempe, the picturesque, authentic Tempe, so precious little now remains, and so very much is gone. Irrecoverably, irredeemably gone. Demolished, destroyed. History, heritage, local flavor, charm, character, ambiance, the original, the individual, and the genuine – all gone. Destroyed, demolished. Building by building, house by house, block upon block, street after street. In an orgy of organized vandalism, old Tempe was swept away, and in its place a new Tempe was created in the image of those colorless dullards who had perpetrated the destruction of the old city and who could now impose the dullness of their minds upon the construction of the new.

In consequence, the city of Tempe became a Disneyfied simulation of itself, a debased counterfeit of what it had been. Pseudo-quaint, fake old west, a falsification and a vulgarization of frontier architecture. (All that is lacking are a few plastic cacti.) Faceless, graceless buildings interspersed with silly, hokey, dorky, kitschy, corny buildings. ("So ugly that even time will never beautify them," as J.B. Priestley says.) Life-sapping bland architecture, structures that starve the eye and starve the spirit. Slick, smooth, synthetic, suggestive of all that is shallow, crass and superficial. Charmless, soulless, dull and impersonal. A city to make you cringe in embarrassment and weep in disbelief. A city that no longer nourishes but numbs the imagination. A city so aesthetically denuded that being there is a form of sensory deprivation.

(And as the famous American architect Louis H. Sullivan once observed: "As you are, so are your buildings; and, as are your buildings, so are you. You and your architecture are the same. Each is the faithful portrait of the other. To read the one is to read the other. To interpret the one is to interpret the other." You may well imagine, then, the inferences to be drawn from the ill-favored buildings that currently blight downtown Tempe.)

What a triumph of boorishness! What a stunning failure of judgement! What a staggering lapse of taste at every level! (I am reminded of the destruction of the Banyan Buddhas by the Taliban.) And from its inception in the early 1970s, this folly took place in the face of persistent opposition from preservationists. Yet as other, wiser cities across the United States increasingly capitalize on their authentic, historical downtowns and districts, (the historic Tucson barrio, to name but one instance) I have the sense that the city government of Tempe, having sucked nearly all of the oxygen out of Tempe and even while continuing to permit the destruction of the last remnants of its past has at length become somewhat uneasy and embarrassed by its disdain for and repudiation of its history, by its reckless, grossly insensitive and singularly ill-advised program of "urban renewal," and now seeks to disguise or deny what really happened.

A plaque on the André Building states that the structure is "one of the last remaining examples of Territorial commercial architecture in Tempe," but fails to note that this is so precisely because successive mayors, city councils and city planners relentlessly demolished all the other examples.

Similarly, Ben Furlong's undeviatingly eulogistic, credulous, booster version of the history of the city, *Tempe: The Past, the Present, and the Future,* a book "made possible by Tempe officials" who provided to Furlong their "help and assistance," (commissioned and published by the City of Tempe?) attempts to gloss over and even to glorify the city's deplorable project of urban destruction, going so far as to assert that in 1971 Tempe "became a city that recognized and sought to preserve its unique history." (p.39) I must say, they certainly chose a unique way of preserving their unique history – by eradicating it. Erroneous claims are likewise set forth by Scott Solliday in his *Tempe Post-World War II Context Study,* which unaccountably asserts that "Tempe has long had an appreciation of its historic buildings." Another fanciful account of Tempe's citycide is recorded in Arizona by Lawrence W. Cheek (Compass American Guides: 1993) in which the author recounts that City Hall rejected a recommendation of "tearing everything down and starting over" in favor of a plan of "respectful renovation" of the historic downtown area. The result of this plan, Cheek contends, was that "Three blocks of handsome turn-of-the-century commercial buildings were restored, not demolished." (p. 151) I only wish it were so, but alas, in a project driven by a supreme lack of vision, in a heartbreaking massacre of the past, those three blocks (and many more besides) of handsome turn-of-the-century buildings *were* demolished, not restored; and alack, nearly everything *was* torn down in order to start over.

From what preposterous premise or prodigious hallucination can such writings possibly have proceeded? Is it the belief of the writers that the present citizens of Tempe cannot grieve for what they do not know has been taken away from them? Are the writers hoping that no-one will notice that the great majority of the city's handsome historic houses and buildings are no longer there?

What was lost in Tempe, together with the many historic buildings and neighborhoods, was the possibility of certain kinds of experience that have value for the life of a city, a nation, or an individual. Authentic, romantic, quirky, qualitative experiences were once – before the destruction of the old city – widely available in Tempe; they were a feature of daily life.

For example, drinking a beer beneath the bullet-riddled ceiling of wonderful old Parry's bar on Mill Avenue was a minor but vivid and vital adventure. Bare, unpretentious Parry's retained still the ambiance of a Wild West saloon. On Sunday afternoons old-timers in hats and suspenders sat on spindle-back wooden chairs to play pinochle at the round wooden tables, and if you sat or stood at the long bar the massive wooden back-bar with its bevelled mirrors and carved American eagles was a pleasure to study. (I was told by the bartender that this masterwork was carved in Ireland, shipped across the Atlantic, sailed through the Panama Canal and transported overland from San Francisco.) Parry's was imbued with a sense of history, of tradition, and of continuity with the pioneer past, as was too the nearby Green Lantern or Pitcher House with its rich brown wood interior and patterned copper ceiling. To buy a buck knife or a woollen watch cap or a pair of levis at the Boston Store was agreeable and satisfying in a way that cannot be communicated to (or even imagined by) those who trade at shopping malls and chain stores or online. It was personal, it was distinctive. A similar quality of experience could be found in making a purchase at Rundle's market. To do so was not a mere routine utilitarian chore (as in a supermarket, a Circle K or Seven-Eleven) but an undertaking that had an intrinsic interest and could be savoured for its own sake, for the premises and furnishings of Rundle's – the vintage beer and dairy case with its thick glass compartments framed by wood, the wooden counter with its large ornamentally embossed metal cash-register, the shelves, the walls and ceilings and linoleum tiled floor – were very attractive and very pleasingly old-fashioned. Sitting at a table by the window eating a bowl of bean soup in the original Restaurant México on Mill Avenue, watching the traffic and the passersby possessed a similar quality, as did browsing for old books in the cluttered, quiet rooms of that large, rambling, gabled Victorian house that stood on the south side of University Avenue between Maple and Ash and served as an antiquarian bookshop. Such places were not contrived, their furnishings were not props placed there to lend atmosphere, these places (and many others like them throughout old Tempe) *had* atmosphere, genuine atmosphere; that was their enduring appeal. Merely being in such places was a pleasure. They were spirit-stirring, heart-exciting. They were as different from the current buildings in Tempe – the ones that have been built in their place – as is natural grass from astro-turf.

Old Tempe with its historic buildings, its leafy streets and handsome old houses, was a place to be cherished, but city officials despised it and destroyed it. It was a place to be preserved, but city officials demolished it, effaced it, erased it, laid waste to it, pulled it down and swept it away. It was a heritage to be honored, valued, respected and passed on, but city officials heedlessly, needlessly cast it away. What a betrayal of stewardship! What aesthetic and historical blindness! What a shameful and short-sighted undertaking!

Inasmuch as a sense of self depends upon a sense of place and a sense of history, and inasmuch as buildings and houses are the irreplaceable repositories of a community's continuity and tradition, the citizens of Tempe are forever impoverished. What then remains to be done? Very little, I'm afraid – the damage is done, the city is irrevocably, irredeemably, irretrievably ruined – but the little that can yet be done is very much worth doing. To protect the last vestiges of old Tempe, the last genuine streets and structures – the south Maple, Ash and Farmer area – the city of Tempe urgently needs a historic preservation ordinance that is utterly uncompromising. In order to ensure the survival of the last distinctive district of the city such an ordinance should be enacted and enforced to serve as a veritable Containment Policy directed against developers. Not another house or plot of ground – not one more – should be yielded to developers. The pitifully little that still remains of real Tempe should be scrupulously shielded and saved, protected and preserved. The alternative to scrupulous preservation is a thoroughly anonymous, homogeneous, de-historicized, flavorless, impersonal and nondescript urban space, a Tempe without spirit or heart, without character or identity, a city blank and faceless, a placeless place.

www.ingramcontent.com/pod-product-compliance
Lightning Source LLC
LaVergne TN
LVHW051443170726
843492LV00002B/514